WHAT DO YOU THINK?

DR. DAVID JEREMIAH

with Dr. David Jeremiah

Edited by: William Kruidenier
Unless otherwise indicated, Scripture verses quoted are from the NEW KING JAMES VERSION.

Printed in the United States of America.

CONTENTS

ABOUT
DR. DAVID JEREMIAH
AND TURNING POINT

D r. David Jeremiah is the founder of Turning Point, a ministry committed to providing Christians with sound Bible teaching relevant to today's changing times through radio and television broadcasts, audio series, books, and live events. Dr. Jeremiah's common-sense teaching on topics such as family, prayer, worship, angels, and biblical prophecy forms the foundation of Turning Point.

David and his wife, Donna, reside in El Cajon, California, where he serves as the senior pastor of Shadow Mountain Community Church. David and Donna have four children and twelve grandchildren.

In 1982, Dr. Jeremiah brought the same solid teaching to San Diego television that he shares weekly with his congregation. Shortly thereafter, Turning Point expanded its ministry to radio. Dr. Jeremiah's inspiring messages can now be heard worldwide on radio, television, and the Internet.

Because Dr. Jeremiah desires to know his listening audience, he travels nationwide holding ministry events that touch the hearts and lives of many people. According to Dr. Jeremiah, "At some point in time, everyone reaches a turning point; and for every person, that moment is unique, an experience to hold onto forever. There's so much changing in today's world that sometimes it's difficult to choose the right path. Turning Point offers people an understanding of God's Word as well as the opportunity to make a difference in their lives."

Dr. Jeremiah has authored numerous books, including *Escape the Coming Night* (Revelation), *The Handwriting on the Wall* (Daniel), *Overcoming Loneliness, God in You* (Holy Spirit), *When Your World Falls Apart, 31 Days to Happiness—Searching for Heaven on Earth, Captured by Grace, What in the World Is Going On?, I Never Thought I'd See the Day!, Agents of the Apocalypse, RESET—Ten Steps to Spiritual Renewal, Ten Questions Christians Are Asking, A Life Beyond Amazing, Perhaps Today, Overcomer,* and *The Book of Signs.*

How to Use This Study Guide

T he purpose of this Turning Point study guide is to reinforce Dr. David Jeremiah's dynamic, in-depth teaching and to aid the reader in applying biblical truth to his or her daily life. This study guide is designed to be used in conjunction with Dr. Jeremiah's *What Do You Think?* audio series, but it may also be used by itself for personal or group study.

Structure of the Lessons

Each lesson is based on one of the messages in the *What Do You Think?* compact disc series and focuses on specific passages in the Bible. Each lesson is composed of the following elements:

- *Outline*

The outline at the beginning of the lesson gives a clear, concise picture of the topic being studied and provides a helpful framework for readers as they listen to Dr. Jeremiah's teaching.

- *Overview*

The overview summarizes Dr. Jeremiah's teaching on the passage being studied in the lesson. Readers should refer to the Scripture passages in their own Bibles as they study the overview. Unless otherwise indicated, Scripture verses quoted are taken from the New King James Version.

- *Personal and Group Application Questions*

This section contains a variety of questions designed to help readers dig deeper into the lesson and the Scriptures, and to apply the lesson to their daily lives. For Bible study groups or Sunday school classes, these questions will provide a springboard for group discussion and interaction.

- *Did You Know?*

This section presents a fascinating fact, historical note, or insight that adds a point of interest to the preceding lesson.

Personal Study

Thank you for selecting *What Do You Think?* for your current study. The lessons in this study guide were created to help you gain fresh insights into God's Word and develop new perspectives on topics you may have previously studied. Each lesson is designed to challenge your thinking, and help you grow in your knowledge of Christ. During your study, it is our prayer that you will discover how biblical truth affects every aspect of your life and your relationship with Christ will be strengthened.

When you commit to completing this study guide, try to set apart a time, daily or weekly, to read through the lessons without distraction. Have your Bible nearby when you read the study guide, so you're ready to look up verses if you need to. If you want to use a notebook to write down your thoughts, be sure to have that handy as well. Take your time to think through and answer the questions. If you plan on reading the study guide with a small group, be sure to read ahead and be prepared to take part in the weekly discussions.

Leader's Guide

Thank you for your commitment to lead a group through *What Do You Think?* Being a leader has its own rewards. You may discover that your walk with the Lord deepens through this experience. Throughout the study guide, your group will explore new topics and review study questions that encourage thought-provoking group discussion.

The lessons in this study guide are suitable for Sunday school classes, small-group studies, elective Bible studies, or home Bible study groups. Each lesson is structured to provoke thought and help you grow in your knowledge and understanding of God. There are multiple components in this section that can help you structure your lessons and discussion time, so make sure you read and consider each one.

Before You Begin

Before you begin each meeting, make sure you and your group are well-versed with the content of the chapter. Every person should have his or her own study guide so they can follow along and write in the study guide if need be. When possible, the study guide should be used with the corresponding compact disc series. You may wish to assign the study guide lesson as homework prior to the meeting of the group and then use the meeting time to listen to the CD and discuss the lesson.

To ensure that everyone has a chance to participate in the discussion, the ideal size for a group is around eight to ten people. If there are more than ten people, try to break up the bigger group into smaller subgroups. Make sure the members are committed to participating each week, as this will help create stability and help you better prepare the structure of the meeting.

At the beginning of the study each week, start the session with a question to challenge group members to think about the issues you will be discussing. The members can answer briefly, but the goal is to have an idea in their mind as you go over the lesson. This allows the group members to become engaged and ready to interact with the group.

After reviewing the lesson, try to initiate a free-flowing discussion. Invite group members to bring questions and insights they may have discovered to the next meeting, especially if they were unsure of the meaning of some parts of the lesson. Be prepared to discuss how biblical truth applies to the world we live in today.

Weekly Preparation

As the group leader, here are a few things you can do to prepare for each meeting:

- Choose whether or not you will play the CD message during your small group session.

  If you decide to play the CD message from Dr. Jeremiah as part of the meeting, you will need to adjust the group time accordingly.

- Make sure you are thoroughly familiar with the material in the lesson.

  Make sure you understand the content of the lesson so you know how to structure group time and you are prepared to lead group discussion.

- Decide, ahead of time, which questions you plan to discuss.

  Depending on how much time you have each week, you may not be able to reflect on every question. Select specific questions which you feel will evoke the best discussion.

- Take prayer requests.

  At the end of your discussion, take prayer requests from your group members and pray for each other.

Structuring the Discussion Time

If you need help in organizing your time when planning your group Bible study, here are two schedules, for sixty minutes and ninety minutes, which can give you a structure for the lesson:

Option 1 (Listen to Audio CD)	60 Minutes	90 Minutes
Welcome: Members arrive and get settled.	N/A	5 minutes
Getting Started Question: Prepares the group for interacting with one another.	Welcome and Getting Started 5 minutes	15 minutes
Message: Listen to the audio CD.	40 minutes	40 minutes
Discussion: Discuss group study questions.	10 minutes	25 minutes
Prayer and Application: Final application for the week and prayer before dismissal.	5 minutes	5 minutes

Option 2 (No Audio CD)	60 Minutes	90 Minutes
Welcome: Members arrive and get settled.	5 minutes	10 minutes
Getting Started Question: Prepares the group for interacting with one another.	10 minutes	10 minutes
Message: Review the lesson.	15 minutes	25 minutes
Discussion: Discuss group study questions.	25 minutes	35 minutes
Prayer and Application: Final application for the week and prayer before dismissal.	5 minutes	10 minutes

As the group leader, it is up to you to keep track of the time and keep things moving along according to your schedule. If your group is having a good discussion, don't feel the need to stop and move on to the next question. Remember, the purpose is to pull together ideas, and share unique insights on the lesson. Make time each week to discuss how to apply these truths to living for Christ today.

The purpose of discussion is for everyone to participate, but don't be concerned if certain group members are more quiet—they may be internally reflecting on the questions and need time to process their ideas before they can share them.

Group Dynamics

Leading a group study can be a rewarding experience for you and your group members—but that doesn't mean there won't be challenges. Certain members may feel uncomfortable discussing topics that they consider very personal, and might be afraid of being called on. Some members might have disagreements on specific issues. To help prevent these scenarios, consider the following ground rules:

- If someone has a question that may seem off topic, suggest that it is discussed at another time, or ask the group if they are okay with addressing that topic.

- If someone asks a question you don't know the answer to, confess that you don't know and move on. If you feel comfortable, invite other group members to give their opinions, or share their comments based on personal experience.

- If you feel like a couple of people are talking much more than others, direct questions to people who may not have shared yet. You could even ask the more dominating members to help draw out the quiet ones.

- When there is a disagreement, encourage the group members to process the matter in love. Invite members from opposing sides to evaluate their opinions and consider the ideas of the other members. Lead the group through Scripture that addresses the topic, and look for common ground.

When issues arise, remind your group to think of Scripture: "Love one another" (John 13:34), "If it is possible, as much as depends on you, live peaceably with all men" (Romans 12:18), and "Be quick to listen, slow to speak and slow to become angry" (James 1:19, NIV).

For Continuing Study

For a complete listing of Dr. Jeremiah's materials for personal and group study call 1-800-947-1993, go online to www.DavidJeremiah.org, or write to Turning Point, P.O. Box 3838, San Diego, CA 92163.

Dr. Jeremiah's *Turning Point* program is currently heard or viewed around the world on radio, television, and the Internet in English. *Momento Decisivo*, the Spanish translation of Dr. Jeremiah's messages, can be heard on radio in every Spanish speaking country in the world. The television broadcast is also broadcast by satellite throughout the Middle East with Arabic subtitles.

Contact Turning Point for radio and television program times and stations in your area, or visit our website at www.DavidJeremiah.org/stationlocator.

WHAT DO YOU THINK?

Gottfried Leibniz (1646-1716) was a German philosopher and mathematician. In one of his last works, he explored the relationship between the brain and the mind. Leibniz's analogy came to be known as "Leibniz's Mill." Leibniz saw a conflict between the mechanical operation of the human brain based on tissue and nerve impulses, and the subjective operations like thinking, sensing, and perceiving that apparently arise from the brain. How can an objective, mechanical organ produce such subjective realities? If the brain could be enlarged to a size that allowed us to walk inside it, he said, like one might walk into the interior of a windmill, we might see nothing more than "parts pushing one another, and never anything by which to explain a perception." So where do love, hate, discernment, longing, dreaming, and perceiving come from?

Neither science nor theology has provided a solution to "Leibniz's Mill." There is still no agreed-upon definition of the mind, though the questions remain: What is the mind? Where is it located? How does it work?

The Bible makes no reference at all to the brain yet refers to the mind more than one hundred times. While the Bible leaves many questions about the mind unanswered, it speaks profoundly about the role of the mind in the spiritual life. In fact, Jesus Christ said the most important thing about the mind recorded in all of Scripture: We are to love God with all our mind (Matthew 22:37).

While Jesus provided no explanation for the mind, it is clear from His words what He meant: We are to use our non-physical abilities to love God. We are to use those abilities that are unique to human beings, created in God's image, in a way that honors God. Human beings were endowed by God with the ability to communicate with Him and with one another at a level that other creatures don't have. While other animals live primarily by instinct, human beings live by choice. We can consider, evaluate, and choose what we think about and how we act on those thoughts. We can choose how we nurture our thought life—what we feed our mind over time. We cannot always choose how and when thoughts arise in our mind, but we can choose whether to accept or reject them. It is with those abilities that Jesus said we should love and honor God—not just with part of our mind but with all our mind. We may not know exactly how to define the mind, but we most certainly know what our mind is capable of. And Jesus said that loving God is the mind's top priority.

It is ironic that the highest part of man—our ability to think and reason with God and one another—has received the least amount of attention from Christians (in spite of Jesus' admonition). Much has been written for Christians about loving God with our physical self (behavior, even our diet and health) and our emotional self (love, hate, and other emotions). But relatively little attention has been given to what it means to love God with all our mind.

What Do You Think? addresses that need from a clear biblical perspective. The study begins by establishing the power of the mind to determine who we are ("As a man thinketh in his heart, so is he"). The challenges of cultivating a devoted, dedicated, diligent, and disciplined mind are covered from key passages of Scripture. Developing a peaceful mind as an antidote to fear and worry is explained, as is the most important concept in spiritual maturity: being spiritually transformed by the renewing of the mind through the Word of God.

YOU ARE NOT WHAT YOU THINK YOU ARE, BUT WHAT YOU THINK, YOU ARE!

Proverbs 23:7

*In this lesson we discover six prerequisites
for loving God with our mind.*

OUTLINE

A beloved idea for Christians is that we become a new creation in Christ. We cherish the idea of a new heart, soul, and spirit. But less emphasis is placed on the mind as part of that new creation. The Christian is responsible for filling his mind with the truth of God in order to love God more.

   I.   **The Priority of a Devoted Mind**

  II.   **The Priority of a Dedicated Mind**

 III.   **The Priority of a Disciplined Mind**

 IV.   **The Priority of a Determined Mind**

  V.   **The Priority of a Discerning Mind**

 VI.   **The Priority of a Developing Mind**

OVERVIEW

James Allen was born in 1864 in England. His father struggled with his business and then was killed in an untimely moment. The ensuing financial crisis forced the 15-year-old James to drop out of school and take a job to help provide for the family. He found a job in a British manufacturing company that he kept until the age of 38—at which point he quit and walked away. He and his wife moved to a small, coastal town in England and lived for 10 years until James' death at age 48. For those 10 years, James' daily habit was to rise before dawn, hike to the top of a nearby hill, meditate for an hour, then return home and devote the morning to writing.

There is no indication that James Allen was a Christian, but one of the twenty books he wrote was based on a verse in Proverbs: "For as he thinks in his heart, so is he. 'Eat and drink!' he says to you, but his heart is not with you." Allen's small book, *As a Man Thinketh*, based on Proverbs 23:7, is credited with giving rise to the self-improvement and positive thinking "industry" that has flourished in the last hundred years.

Allen's point was simple: Our thoughts are the most important thing about us. What we accomplish, or fail to accomplish, is a direct result of how we think. He wrote,

> Good thoughts and actions can never produce bad results; and bad thoughts and actions can never produce good results. And this is but saying that nothing can come from corn but corn, nothing from nettles but nettles. Men understand this law in the natural world, and they work with it; but few understand it in the moral world (though its operation is just as simple and undeviating).[1]

Our lives follow the train of our thoughts. An angry person thinks angry thoughts, a negative person thinks negative thoughts, a positive person thinks positive thoughts, and so on. The mind is like a garden that must be cultivated—and we are the gardeners:

> A person's mind may be likened to a garden which may be intelligently cultivated or allowed to run wild; but whether cultivated or neglected, it must and will bring forth fruit. If the useful seeds are not put into the garden, an abundance of useless seeds will fall upon it and will continue to produce their fruit.[2]

This is consistent with the law of harvest found in Galatians 6:7: "Do not be deceived, God is not mocked; for whatever a man sows, that he will also reap."

While Proverbs 23:7 is a truth from God's Word, the verse has been used to promote many unscriptural ideas. The "positive mental attitude" industry (which has Christian versions) teaches that "whatever the mind can conceive and the heart believe, you can achieve." But that is not what the verse teaches. We do not have the power to think things into existence or to think our way to success. But the Bible does teach that our thoughts are important and that our thoughts influence our life.

The power of one's thoughts was illustrated in the experience of the prophet Elijah. When Elijah challenged the faith of the prophets of Baal on Mount Carmel (1 Kings 18), he experienced a tremendous victory. It was, literally and figuratively, a mountaintop experience for Elijah. But, as often happens following a moment of victory, Elijah experienced the opposite—a "death valley" moment. When Queen Jezebel heard that Elijah had killed all her prophets, she was furious and swore to kill Elijah. He went from exhilaration to depression, and fled for his life into the wilderness.

If you read Elijah's story in the Old Testament, you will find he felt worthless, hopeless, isolated, and suicidal. He wanted to die to escape the pursuing Jezebel. But God met with Elijah in the wilderness and helped him regain his strength and his perspective. He reminded Elijah that he wasn't the only faithful prophet, that he wasn't defeated, and that God still wanted to use him. And Elijah was restored. Elijah's problem wasn't Jezebel. What could Jezebel have done against Almighty God? Elijah's problem was between his ears—his thoughts.

The human brain, the center of our thinking, is a profound organ:

The human brain's twelve to fourteen billion cells are only a shadow of its complexity, for each cell sends out thousands of connecting tendrils so that a single cell may be connected with 10,000 neighboring cells, each of which is constantly exchanging data impulses. These twelve to fourteen billion brain cells times 10,000 connectors make the human mind an unparalleled computer. The mind's activity has been compared to 1,000 switchboards, each big enough to serve New York City, all running at full speed as they receive and send questions and orders. Put another way, there is more electronic equivalent in one human brain than in all the radio and television stations of the entire world put together. The human brain does not miss a thing. It's capable of giving and receiving the subtlest input— from imagining a universe in which time bends, to creating the polyphonic texture of a Bach fugue, or transmitting and receiving a message from God—a feat that no computer could ever accomplish.[3]

In this lesson we will look at six priorities concerning the mind —six ways to keep our thoughts headed in a direction that will help us accomplish God's best for our life.

THE PRIORITY OF A DEVOTED MIND

Jesus included the mind in His list of ways to "love the Lord your God" in Matthew 22:37. Besides loving God with our heart and soul, we are to love Him with our mind as well. But what does that mean?

First, it means acknowledging that the mind is important. Unfortunately, many Christians put all their emphasis on being guided by the Spirit to the exclusion of the mind. They say the best way to use the mind is to put it in neutral so as not to influence what the Spirit of God might want to say or do. "Mindless Christianity" is a negative term used to criticize some parts of modern evangelical Christianity where anti-intellectual priorities have ruled the day. Too many people think the mind is the enemy of the heart, but that is not a biblical point of view. Paul said, "Whatever you do, do all to the glory of God" (1 Corinthians 10:31), and that certainly includes thinking with our mind.

Many people take the perspective of the Tin Woodman in *The Wonderful Wizard of Oz*: "I shall take the heart," said the Tin Woodman, "for brains do not make one happy and happiness is the best thing in the world."[4] To prefer the heart over the mind is an artificial choice. Both are gifts of God to be used in loving Him for His glory.

Benjamin B. Warfield was a great theologian who taught for 35 years at Princeton Seminary. His statement on the battle between the heart and mind is one of the best I have ever read:

Sometimes we hear it said that ten minutes on your knees will give you a truer, deeper, more operative knowledge of God than ten hours over your books. But why should you turn from God when you turn to your books, or feel that you must turn from your books in order to turn to God? . . . Put your heart into your studies; do not merely occupy your mind with them, but put your heart into them. They will bring you daily and hourly into the very presence of God.[5]

Whether one is a seminary student or a student of aerodynamics, medicine, marketing, or building construction—if one is a Christian he should put both his heart and mind into his studies. When we study, we should put our heart into it; and when we worship, we should put our mind into it. The Christian life is never the heart versus the mind! We are to love God with the passions of the heart and the rigor of the mind: "You shall love the Lord your God with all your heart, with all your soul, and with all your mind" (Matthew 22:37).

THE PRIORITY OF A DEDICATED MIND

Philippians 2:5 says, "Let this mind be in you which was also in Christ Jesus." And 1 Corinthians 2:16 reminds us, "For 'who has known the mind of the Lord that he may instruct Him?' But we have the mind of Christ."

Having the mind of Christ, or the same mind "which was also in Christ Jesus" does not make us God. It simply means to look at life through the mind's-eye of the Savior—through His values, desires, and priorities. It means to use the gift of the mind in the way Jesus would, to think like God thinks instead of like the world thinks. Kent Hughes, whom I quoted previously in describing the mind, offers this perspective on the mind of Christ:

> The dizzying potential of the human mind reaches its apex in the possibility of possessing the mind of Christ through the ministry of the Holy Spirit—a possibility affirmed by Paul when he said, 'We have the mind of Christ.' No computer will ever be able to think God's thoughts nor will any device ever be able to know the heart of God or do His works. But the mystery which resides between our ears has this capacity. It was created for this very purpose—to have the mind of Christ.[6]

THE PRIORITY OF A DISCIPLINED MIND

First Peter 1:13 says, "Therefore gird up the loins of your mind, be sober, and rest your hope fully upon the grace that is to be brought to you at the revelation of Jesus Christ." And in 2 Corinthians 10:5, Paul reveals that the mind is the primary battleground of spiritual warfare. We are to cast down thoughts that argue against the knowledge of God, "bringing every thought into captivity to the obedience of Christ."

"Girding up" is a term from ancient military training. Soldiers were taught to use their belt as a place to tie up their robe to keep it out of their way in combat. So when Peter says we are to gird up our mind, he means we are to prepare our mind for battle; we are to be ready for spiritual warfare.

It's all about focus. We are to rid our mind of the extraneous and irrelevant things that keep us occupied and distracted from what is really important. We are to identify those things that keep us from making progress in the knowledge of God and service of God and bring them all "into captivity to the obedience of Christ." We are to be proactive. We are not to wander aimlessly through life allowing our mind to be filled and occupied with the things of this world. Our mind is to be under our control. We are the sole gatekeeper for our mind. Nothing can get in and take up residence without our permission. And once there, nothing can remain unless we allow it. Our goal should be to monitor our thoughts with a sanctified screen that is sensitive to what will move us forward with God and what will hold us back.

Oswald Chambers wrote, "God will not make me think like Jesus. I have to do it by myself. I have to bring every thought into captivity to the obedience of Christ."[7] I recall the proactive stance my father took when I was very young and televisions were just becoming common in American homes. Whenever something he thought was objectionable came on the screen—such as an alcohol or tobacco commercial—my father would get up and change the channel or turn the volume down. As we children got older, we would act as the remote control for my father. He would tell us to get up and change the channel or turn the TV off when something inappropriate came on. He didn't want his children's minds to be filled with words and images that he knew would not move us in the right direction in life.

I shudder to imagine what my father would think about the things that are on television today, and how most Christians take in that content without objection. It is up to us to stay focused and be proactive about what we allow to find a home in our mind.

THE PRIORITY OF A DETERMINED MIND

In Colossians 3:2, Paul writes, "Set your mind on things above, not on things on the earth." This idea continues from the previous point—it is our responsibility to "set" our mind on godly things. (In the Greek language, the verb form of "set your mind" is an imperative command; it is a command, not a suggestion that is optional.)

Paul describes what we *are* to set our mind on ("things above") and what we *are not* ("things on the earth"). The choice and the power to make that choice are ours. The father of the Protestant Reformation, Martin Luther, is said to have observed that we cannot prevent the birds from flying overhead, but we can prevent them from making a nest in our hair. We cannot always keep from hearing or seeing things that become thoughts in our mind, but we can choose not to meditate on those things and allow them to become part of our consciousness and therefore our life.

If Jesus Christ is truly Lord of all, then He must also be Lord over our mind. That means our mind and our thoughts must be subject to His Lordship. Our mind must be used for His glory, for carrying out His desires for our life. To call Jesus "Lord" and then use our mind for that which is an offense to Him is inconsistent. As biblical Christians we put great emphasis on the truth of 2 Corinthians 5:17—that we are "a new creation" in Christ, that "all things have become new." Surely that includes our mind. We have been given the Spirit-led ability to think new thoughts and pursue new ideas consistent with the kingdom of God. It is a sad fact that many Christians look new on the outside but possess a mind still set on the things of this world.

THE PRIORITY OF A DISCERNING MIND

In Paul's most specific passage on *what* we should think about, he writes,

"Finally, brethren, whatever things are true, whatever things are noble, whatever things are just, whatever things are pure, whatever things are lovely, whatever things are of good report, if there is any virtue and if there is anything praiseworthy—meditate on these things." (Philippians 4:8)

The context of that verse is important. Paul was writing about fear and anxiety. In the two previous verses he exhorted them to commit their worries and fears to God through prayer, reminding them that God's peace would become a guard for their mind (Philippians 4:6-7). But then he added the exhortation in verse 8: What you think about will make a difference. You can't expect to have a peaceful life if you are continually thinking about negative, fearful, worrisome things. In using a group of adjectives—true, noble, just, pure, lovely, good report, virtuous, praiseworthy—it is like He is describing God Himself. If we focus on God and realities that reflect who God is, peace will come, and peace will remain with us. Thinking about God's attributes and His promises, the works and faithfulness of God in the past, the blessings of God in the present . . . all those thoughts will give us peace about the future.

When we are tempted to think about unsettling things, the key is not to say, "I refuse to think about that!" Everyone knows that doesn't work—it only causes that unsettling thought to become even more deeply settled in our mind. Instead, we must replace fear and insecurity and worry with thoughts that are true, noble, just, pure, and so on. When we fill our mind with those thoughts, the negative thoughts have to flee as they are crowded out by positive and edifying thoughts.

THE PRIORITY OF A DEVELOPING MIND

This last point is perhaps the most important of all—it has the most long-term implications: It is possible to develop the mind. Or, in the words of Paul in Romans 12:2, it is possible (and our responsibility) to "renew" the mind: "And do not be conformed to this world, but be transformed by the renewing of your mind, that you may prove what is that good and acceptable and perfect will of God."

The world around us is continually exerting pressure on us to become like it in our thoughts and our actions (1 John 5:19). The most well-known translation of Romans 12:2 is by the British translator J. B. Phillips in *The New Testament in Modern English*. He translated Romans 12:2 this way: "Don't let the world around you squeeze you into its own mould, but let God re-mould your minds from within, so that you may prove in practice that the plan of God for you is good, meets all his demands and moves towards the goal of true maturity."

Instead of the world squeezing our mind into its mold from the outside, we must allow God to re-mold our mind from within. In terminology from the computer age, we must allow God to re-program our mind to think thoughts consistent with Him and His kingdom. That is the only way to discover and live out the "good and acceptable and perfect will of God." It is by the renewing of our mind that the Holy Spirit conforms us to the image of Christ and we develop what Paul calls "the mind of Christ." No one will grow in godliness whose mind is not continually being transformed from within by the Spirit of God. And the Spirit's key tool in that transformation is the Word of God. As we learn, memorize, and meditate on the truth of God's Word, we begin to think God's thoughts after Him and our mind is renewed. But it doesn't happen overnight. The renewing of our mind is a lifelong process that moves us ever closer to being conformed to the image of Christ (Romans 8:29).

David wrote in Psalm 119:11, "Your word I have hidden in my heart, that I might not sin against You." By filling his heart and mind with the word of God, David was kept from sin. And when we are kept from sin, we become more like Christ, the One who never sinned. So becoming more like Him begins with the Word of God renewing our mind so that we walk in a manner pleasing to God.

Renewal suggests change. If our mind is continually being renewed, we will continually be changed from the likeness of our fallen, sinful self into the likeness of Jesus Christ. As old, carnal thoughts are replaced by new, godly thoughts, we will take on the characteristics of what (and Who) we are thinking and meditating about. And there is a cumulative effect—the more we fill our mind with godly thoughts, the less inclination we will have to think otherwise. But it must be a continual effort on our part. The unrelenting force of this world, working to conform us to its own image never stops. If we are not challenging that conformation process, we will never be transformed. It is not the natural state of fallen human beings to think godly thoughts. Therefore, to begin the process of renewal seems like an uphill battle, and it is. But by the power of the indwelling Spirit, renewal and transformation become a Christ-like way of life.

More than any other means, continual meditation on the Word of God is what the Spirit uses to renew our mind and transform us. Thus Paul wrote, "Let the word of Christ dwell in you richly in all wisdom, teaching and admonishing one another in psalms and hymns and spiritual songs, singing with grace in your hearts to the Lord" (Colossians 3:16). Every time we are exposed to the transforming truth of the Word of God—in sermons, hymns, discussions in Bible studies, reading biblically-based books and literature, and especially in the quiet of our own Bible study—we are giving the Holy Spirit what He will use to transform us.

The more of God's Word that fills your mind, the more you will love God with your mind—and vice versa. Think about how much of God's Word is filling your mind on a daily and weekly basis and purpose to increase it so you can love God with *all* your mind.

Notes

1. James Allen, *As a Man Thinketh* (New York, Barnes & Noble Books, 2002), 22.

2. Ibid, 11.

3. R. Kent Hughes, *Disciplines of a Godly Man* (Wheaton, IL: Crossway Books, 1991), 71.

4. L. Frank Baum, *The Wonderful Wizard of Oz* (New York: Dover, 1960), 57-58, 61.

5. "The Religious Life of Theological Students," B. B. Warfield at Princeton Theological Seminary, October 4, 1911.

6. Hughes, op cit, 71.

7. Oswald Chambers, *My Utmost for His Highest* (New York: Dodd, Mead and Company, 1935), 166 (reading for June 14).

1. Read Matthew 22:37.

    a. What does it means to love the Lord "with all your mind"?

    b. Why is it important to love the Lord with the heart, the soul and the mind together?

    c. What hard or sacrificial choice(s) might a Christian need to make in order to love God this way?

d. What does it say about the quality of one's love for the Lord if there is an unwillingness to make sacrifices in the name of the Lord?

e. Why is it easier to hide one's love for God with the mind than with the body? How does the body ultimately reveal the state of the mind when it comes to godliness?

2. In Philippians 2:5, we are called to "let this mind" be in us just as it was in Christ.

   a. In practical terms, what does this mean?

   b. How should a Christian go about obeying this command of Scripture?

b. If we are obeying Ephesians 5:18, why will we also be obeying Philippians 2:5?

c. What is the best way you have found to let the mind (the Word) of Christ dwell in you? (Colossians 3:16) In contrast, what hinders your ability to let Christ dwell in you?

1. As a group, discuss the six priorities that concern the mind. Then share which priority you need to focus on more and why.

   a. A devoted mind

   b. A dedicated mind

   c. A disciplined mind

d. A determined mind

e. A discerning mind

f. A developing mind

2. Paul states in 2 Corinthians 10:1-5 that our mind is the epicenter for spiritual warfare. Therefore, in what way does the command to "gird up the loins of your mind" (1 Peter 1:13) prepare you for battle?

a. In what way is the mind considered a weapon to be used in spiritual warfare?

b. How are we to care for the mind, in order to maintain its weaponry?

3. Read Colossians 3:2, and discuss the following questions:

   a. What does Paul mean by "things above"?

   b. Are you currently setting your mind on godly things, or earthly things?

   c. According to Philippians 4:8, what things are we specifically to set our mind on? (Hint: "Whatever things are.")

d. Why is it important to mediate on these godly things?

e. Discuss ways we can we fill our minds with godly things (truth, nobility, justice, etc.) instead of earthly things (greed, envy, covetousness)? Write down the suggestions that apply to you personally.

Throughout history, thinkers have struggled to identify and define the mind—a problem known as the mind-body problem. The brain is easily identified as a physical organ located in the human head, but no such location for the mind of man has been identified. The Bible mentions the mind just over one hundred times without defining or locating it—and never mentions the brain. Therefore, the ancients likely used the word *mind* to refer to the brain —what they perceived as the seat of thought. Scripture assumes an understanding that the presence of the mind is demonstrated by thoughts, reasoning, consciousness, judgment, and perception. But exactly where the brain ends and the mind begins remains a mystery.

THE PRIORITY OF A DEVOTED MIND

Matthew 22:37

*In this lesson we discover four ways
to love God with all our mind.*

OUTLINE

Becoming a Christian can be compared to moving to a foreign country where everything—culture, language, education—is different. We begin a lifelong process of replacing the prior thoughts and patterns of life with those of our new home—a process that is centered in the mind.

   I.   **When We Feed on His Word**

  II.   **When We Find God's Wisdom**

 III.   **When We Follow God's Will**

 IV.   **When We Fight God's War**

OVERVIEW

Human beings are classified scientifically as *homo sapiens*—"thinking (wise, rational) beings." Non-human animals do not have the ability to think on a par with human beings, due to humans having been created in the image of God (Genesis 1:26-27). God created human beings to be His representatives on earth, to have dominion and stewardship over the earth, and to communicate with Him face-to-face. To accomplish those purposes God gave humans a unique mind, one that allows us to do only what humans can do—talk to God: "'Come now, and let us reason together,' says the Lord" (Isaiah 1:18).

The Christian's mind is different from the fallen human mind in that we have, by the presence of the Holy Spirit, the "mind of Christ" (1 Corinthians 2:16). That means we are able to think in a manner that glorifies God, to think the thoughts of God after Him. It is with the redeemed mind, the born-again mind, the mind of the new creation (2 Corinthians 5:17), that we are to love God: "Jesus said to him, 'You shall love the lord your God with all your heart, with all your soul, and with all your mind'" (Matthew 22:37).

Jesus' words were based on the words of Deuteronomy 6:5: "You shall love the Lord your God will all your heart, with all your soul, and with all your strength." Jesus added the word "mind" to His quotation of Deuteronomy 6:5. (Some Greek copies of the Hebrew Old Testament included the word "mind" in their version of Deuteronomy 6:5—of which Jesus would have been aware—and so He added it to His quotation of the verse. Mark's version of Jesus' words includes all four dimensions: heart, soul, mind, and strength [Mark 12:30].)

The important thing to note is Jesus' recognition of the importance of loving God with our mind as well as with our heart, soul, and strength. It affirms the importance of being a good steward of the gift of thinking, rationality, and wisdom. The great British apologist C. S. Lewis wrote, "If you're thinking of becoming a Christian, I warn you, you are embarking on something which is going to take the whole of you—brains and all."[1] And he was right!

Our goal in this lesson is to explore the idea of loving God with *all* our mind, from four points of view. We love God with our mind . . .

WHEN WE FEED ON HIS WORD

There is no better way to love God with our mind than to feed on His Word. The Bible contains God's very words to us. What could be a better tool for renewing our mind than to meditate on the words that came from the mind of God Himself?

The best place in Scripture to meditate on the power of God's Word is Psalm 119—the longest psalm (and chapter) in the Bible. Four verses from Psalm 119 capture the essence of the entire psalm:

Oh, how I love Your law!

It is my meditation all the day.

You, through Your commandments, make me wiser
than my enemies;

For they are ever with me.

I have more understanding than all my teachers,

For Your testimonies are my meditation.

I understand more than the ancients,

Because I keep Your precepts.

(Psalm 119:97-100)

Nearly all of the 176 verses in the psalm contain a reference, in the form of a synonym, to God's Word: law, testimonies, ways, precepts, statutes, commandments, judgments, ordinances, and so on. And the psalm is filled with action words that indicate how we are to relate to God's Word: We should walk in it, keep it, seek it, look into it, learn it, take heed to it, hide it in our heart, rejoice in it, meditate on it, contemplate it, remember it, strengthen yourself according to it, get the understanding of it, incline your heart to it, be revived in it, never forget it, be taught from it, consider it, direct your steps according to it, and get understanding from it.

We cannot be changed by that which we do not know. To be changed by God, we must know God's Word. When our mind is filled with the words God has given to us in the Bible, we can be shaped by those words. It's impossible to love God with all our mind while ignoring the Bible.

Dietrich Bonhoeffer was a young Lutheran pastor in Germany when Adolf Hitler was making his rise to power. When Hitler placed the Lutheran (state) church under his control, Bonhoeffer resisted and refused to align with Hitler's condemnation of the Jewish people. So he became a marked man in the eyes of the Third Reich. On a visit to America for inspiration and guidance on what he should do, he visited an African-American church in New York City where he encountered a faith more vibrant than any he had ever witnessed. And his life was changed forever. He returned to Germany with a personal relationship with God and a newfound love for God's Word. He began to immerse himself in the teachings of Scripture:

First of all, I will confess quite simply—I believe that the Bible alone is the answer to all of our questions, and that we need only to ask repeatedly and a little humbly, in order to receive this answer. One cannot simply read the Bible like other books. One must be prepared really to enquire of it. Only thus will it reveal itself. Only if we expect from it the ultimate answer, shall we receive it. And that is because in the Bible God speaks to us. And one cannot simply think about God in one's own strength. One has to enquire of Him. Only if we seek Him will He answer us . . . . Just as we do not grasp the words of someone we love by taking them to bits, but by simply receiving them, so that for days they go on lingering in our minds, simply because they are the words of a person we love. And just as those words reveal more and more of that person who said them as we go on . . . so it will be with the words of the Bible. Only if we will venture to enter into the words of the Bible, as though in them, this God were speaking to us Who loves us and does not will to leave us, only so shall we learn to rejoice in the Bible.

Further, Bonheoffer said,

I would like to tell you now quite personally: since I have begun to read the Bible in this way—and this has not been for so very long—it becomes more wonderful to me. I read it in the morning and in the evening, often during the day as well. And every day I consider a text which I have chosen for the whole week and try to sink deeply into it so as really to hear what it is saying. And I know that without this I could not live properly any longer.[2]

Bonhoeffer was ultimately hanged for his resistance to Hitler, but not before leaving a legacy of the power of God's Word to strengthen and change one's life.

As young lovers do when they treasure the letters they receive from each other, pouring over them time and again (as my wife and I did when we were engaged), so our love for God with our mind will move us to pour over His Word until we think His thoughts after Him.

The second way we love God with our mind is . . .

WHEN WE FIND GOD'S WISDOM

Proverbs 3:13 says, "Happy is the man who finds wisdom, and the man who gains understanding" (see also Proverbs 3:16-18; 8:11; 16:16). Wisdom is searchable and findable!

What is the difference between wisdom and knowledge? To use an example from our digital age, your computer's hard drive may be filled with information (knowledge), but it takes a software application to retrieve and order and help you use that information. So knowledge is information, but the ability to use and apply that information is wisdom.

The Bible is full of information—words. But without wisdom, the information will never achieve its potential and intended result. Wisdom is the ability to take the Word of God and apply it to the life you are living. In the ancient Hebrew language, wisdom meant "skill." So wisdom means developing the skill to live life from God's perspective, to use the information God has given us in all the various areas of our life. Wisdom is doing the right thing without a precedent, facing a brand new situation, and using God's Word to create a way forward. It is sensing, as a result of years of exposure to God's ways, words, and will, what God would have us do in a given moment. Living a life with wisdom (skill), based on filling our mind with God's Word, is a way to love God with all our mind.

A Mennonite pastor named Shane Hipps, who was a strategic planner in the advertising industry before entering the ministry, has written a book, *Flickering Pixels*, on how the Internet impacts our life. In an interview with *Christianity Today* magazine he said,

> The Internet created a permanent puberty of the mind. We get locked into so much information and the inability to sort that information meaningfully limits our capacity to understand. The last stage of knowledge is wisdom. But we are miles from wisdom because the Internet encourages the opposite of what creates wisdom. And what is that? Stillness,

time and inefficient things like suffering. On the Internet, there is no such thing as waiting; there is no such thing as stillness. There is just constant churning.[3]

The Internet is filled with information but is missing the ingredients that turn information into wisdom. I believe there is great wisdom in this perspective on the Internet!

I am certainly not against technology—a large part of Turning Point's ministry is technology driven, and I thank God for the advances that allow us to get the Word of God out all over the world. But we have to be very careful that we don't lose sight of those things that create wisdom in our life—time, reflection, experience, correction, and meditation upon God's Word. We need information, but after that, we don't need *more* information. We need to allow God the opportunity to create wisdom in our life. And it takes discipline in our digital age to turn off the electronics long enough to process the knowledge we already have.

The apostle Paul wrote to Timothy: "Consider what I say, and may the Lord give you understanding in all things" (2 Timothy 2:7). "Consider" is the key word, for it is with the mind that Timothy (and we) would think about what Paul communicated to him. Thinking and understanding go together. It is from thinking, considering, praying—all activities of the mind—that we gain understanding. The Spirit of God in us gives us wisdom and understanding as we think about (consider) what God has said.

James even wrote that we should ask God for wisdom and understanding when we are in need of it: "If any of you lacks wisdom, let him ask of God, who gives to all liberally and without reproach, and it will be given to him" (James 1:5). Very simply, we pray, "Lord, help me know how to apply your Word in this situation I am facing."

The third way we love God with our mind is . . .

WHEN WE FOLLOW GOD'S WILL

Romans 12:1-2 clearly links the Christian's mind with the Christian's pursuit of God's perfect will: "And do not be conformed to this world, but be transformed by the renewing of your mind, that you may prove what is that good and acceptable and perfect will of God."

God's will is not only "good and acceptable," it is also "perfect." God has a perfect and unique will for you, a will He has been communicating and working out in us from the earliest days of our life. God exhorted fathers in Israel to communicate His laws and precepts to their children from the time they were children (Deuteronomy 6:6-7). Loving God with all their mind started at an early age for Jewish children as they took in the details of God's will expressed through His Word.

But discovering God's will comes not only through knowing God's Word. It also comes by parents modeling the words and will of God for their children. Having a family devotional time for a few minutes each day is important, but the rest of the day and night are important too. The Word of God is to be integrated into every moment of the day so that children discover how to apply it to life. Children need to see their parents manifest wisdom and understanding by applying the Word to the unplanned moments in life. Children learn to live life skillfully by observing how their parents do it. They learn the Word of God in an informational sense during family devotions, then learn wisdom as God allows situations to arise where walking by faith is a necessity.

Moses told the people, "Hear, O Israel: The Lord our God, the Lord is one!" (Deuteronomy 6:4). Having one God was in stark contrast to what the Hebrews had learned in Egypt where there were numerous gods who were often in conflict with one another. But with the God of Israel and Christianity, there is only one true God. There is only one perfect will to pursue. And you can know God's perfect will for your life by loving Him with all your mind.

And that is true regardless of where God's will leads you. Whatever your calling or vocation, God wants you to apply all your mental faculties to the pursuit of His will for your life. Regardless of who you are or what your abilities are or what your calling is, every one of us is expected to love God with *all* our mind. Work on Monday is no different than church on Sunday. We are not to love God with our mind only on Sunday, then turn our mind off from Monday through Saturday. All of our week and all of our mind are to reflect our love for God. Being the most creative and best engineer, plumber, parent, grandparent, athlete, student— whatever our calling—is just as important as being the best pastor one can be. We are to love God with all our mind in any and every situation in life.

We find God's "good and acceptable and perfect will" in life by the continual process of renewing our mind through the Word of God. Our mind is transformed into the will of God instead of being conformed to the will of this world. The more we engage in that process, the clearer God's will for us becomes—and the less likely we are to be distracted by the pressures of this world that seek to inhibit our transformation into the image of Christ. When we stay focused on doing God's will daily, we realize that we are living out God's perfect will for our life.

The fourth way we love God with our mind is . . .

WHEN WE FIGHT GOD'S WAR

A key theme in the New Testament is that spiritual warfare is not fought as earthly wars are fought—"according to the flesh." Rather, "the weapons of our warfare are not carnal but mighty in God for pulling down strongholds, casting down arguments and every high thing that exalts itself against the knowledge of God, *bringing every thought into captivity to the obedience of Christ*" (2 Corinthians 10:3-5, emphasis added). Spiritual warfare is fought on the battlefield of the mind. Every thought or idea that exalts itself against God must be taken captive to the obedience of Christ. This is the same idea expressed by Peter: "Always be ready to give a defense to everyone who asks you a reason for the hope that is in you" (1 Peter 3:15). A defense is a well-reasoned answer—using the mind to defeat untruths concerning God and faith in Him.

As never before in U.S. history, Christianity is under attack. For example, the doctrine that Jesus is the only way to God (John 14:6; Acts 4:12) is considered intolerant and politically incorrect! But it is what the Bible says. Jesus said the way to the kingdom of heaven is straight and difficult, not broad, and that there will be relatively few who are willing to walk in that way (Matthew 7:13-14). That is not a popular message, and we must know how to defend it. It is not just for scholars to study the defense of the faith. Peter said that every Christian should be "ready to give a defense," and that means reading and studying and learning—all activities of the mind. The mind must be engaged in order to promote and defend the faith. The primary battlefield for spiritual warfare is always the battlefield of the mind where thoughts compete against one another. And our mind must be filled with the biblical defenses of the faith.

So, we love God four ways: feeding on His Word, finding His wisdom, following His will, and fighting His war. In the cultural war against Christianity, we can defend our faith by learning to respond to the questions of seekers and the attacks of opponents of

Christ. C. S. Lewis, addressing a group of Christian students at Oxford University, said:

> If all the world were Christian, it might not matter if the entire world were educated. But, as it is, a cultural life will exist outside the church whether it exists inside or not. To be ignorant and simple—not to be able to meet the enemies on their own ground—would be to throw down our weapons, and to betray our uneducated brethren who have, under God, no defense against the intellectual attacks of the heathen.[4]

Lewis says it is the responsibility of us all to use the knowledge and education we have—to engage the culture in the realm of the mind—to defend the faith against attackers. Whatever "mind" you have—that is, whatever level of knowledge and education you possess—that is what God wants you to use to persuade others of their need for Christ. Not to do so is to allow the culture's arguments to gain the upper hand in their attack against the supremacy of God in all creation. God has given us a Spirit-empowered mind and truth-based wisdom to defend our faith on the basis of biblical truth.

General William K. Harrison was the most decorated soldier in the 30th Infantry Division in World War II, receiving every medal for valor, including the Purple Heart, except the Congressional Medal of Honor. Because of his character he was asked by President Eisenhower to lead the long negotiations that ultimately ended the Second World War.

While a student at West Point, William Harrison began a discipline that lasted the rest of his life. He read the Old Testament through once each year and the New Testament through *four times* each year. And he kept it up throughout his hectic and dangerous career as a soldier. At the age of 90, when his failing eyesight prevented General Harrison from continuing to read, he had completed 70 readings of the Old Testament and 280 readings of the New Testament. It is no wonder that, for 18 years, he lead the Officers Christian Fellowship, a Christian organization for military personnel.[5]

There are more than a few lessons to draw from the life of General Harrison. Most important is the idea that we don't have time to read God's Word. If it's possible to lead armies on the battlefield and negotiate peace treaties between nations, and still read the Bible daily, then anything is possible! None of us are busier than General Harrison was. Second, others will recognize the transformation in our life that will come from loving God with our mind. Everyone around General Harrison recognized his unique character. And thirdly, we will gain wisdom for handling the complicated situations life throws at us. We may not have to bring warring nations to terms, but we will face matters that seem just as challenging. And wisdom will win the day if our mind has been transformed by the Word of God.

Start where you are today—set aside your mind as holy unto God, for His pleasure and glory, by filling it with His Word.

Notes

1. C. S. Lewis, *Mere Christianity* (San Francisco, CA: Harpers, 2001), 78.

2. Eric Metaxas, *Bonhoeffer: Pastor, Martyr, Prophet, Spy* (Nashville, TN: Thomas Nelson, Publishing, 2010), 136-137.

3. Interview by Mark Galli, "From the Printing Press to the iPhone," *Christianity Today* magazine, http://www.christianitytoday.com/ct/2009/may/20.64.html, 06 May 2009, (accessed 21 October 2010).

4. Gene Edward Veith, *Loving God with All Your Mind: Thinking as a Christian in the Postmodern World* (Wheaton, IL: Crossway Books, 1987), 153.

5. Cited by R. Kent Hughes and Bryan Chapell, *Preaching the Word - 1 & 2 Timothy and Titus, - To Guard the Deposit* (Downers Grove, IL: Crossway Books, 2000), 109.

1. Read Psalm 119:97-100.

   a. List the three categories of people whom the psalmist says he has become wiser than:

      1. Verse 98:

         The reason:

      2. Verse 99:

         The reason:

      3. Verse 100:

         The reason:

b. Practically speaking, what does the psalmist mean in verse 97 by saying God's Word is his "meditation all the day"? How is this similar to "pray without ceasing" in 1 Thessalonians 5:17? How does one meditate all day and pray without ceasing?

2. If the root meaning of wisdom is "skill," and understanding is "discernment," why do you think one would become "happy" as described in Proverbs 3:13?

a. How might failure to possess moral skill and discernment lead to unhappiness in life?

b. Discuss the value of spiritual discernment and wisdom in the Christian's life.

3. Read Proverbs 3:16-18.

   a. Who is the female subject (her, she) of these verses? (see Proverbs 3:13)

b. Do all wise people live peaceful, pleasant, long lives? (verses 17-18) If not, what is the intent of these verses? (Hint: Who is likely to live a longer, more peaceful, life? A wise man or a fool?)

c. Proverbs 3:13-15; 8:11; 16:16 compare wisdom and great wealth. Why would a person be richer with wisdom than with silver, gold, and precious jewels? What can wisdom provide that money can't buy?

1. Read 2 Timothy 2:7, Proverbs 2:1-6, and James 1:5.

   a. How do Paul's words to Timothy compare with Proverbs 2:6 in reference to God giving wisdom?

   b. What prerequisites do you find in Proverbs 2:1-5 for the Lord to provide wisdom? (Note the occurrence of "if" in verses 1, 3, and 4, and "then" in verse 5.)

   c. How do verses 2-4 suggest effort or exertion on our part in the gaining of wisdom?

d. How does Proverbs 2:3 parallel James 1:5? How does that put the responsibility for gaining wisdom on us?

2. Discuss the concept of the "renewing of your mind" as found in Romans 12:2.

a. How is studying, knowing, and applying God's Word a way of renewing the mind?

b. In what way is the mind linked to our Christian pursuit of obtaining God's "perfect will" for our life?

c. How are we capable of loving God with all our mind? (Matthew 22:37) How does our love for Him manifest itself in knowledge and wisdom as we seek out his "perfect will"?

3. Within the group, pair up and pray for one another. Ask the Lord to bestow you with wisdom, and knowledge. And pray that you may faithfully renew your mind so that you can fervently seek His will.

Psalm 119 is one of the most artistically amazing passages in the Bible because of its acrostic structure. Acrostic poems can be structured in different ways, but they all follow a pattern of beginning a verse or verses with successive letters of the Hebrew alphabet. Psalm 119 divides its 176 verses into groups of eight verses. All the verses in group one begin with *aleph*, the first letter of the Hebrew alphabet, the next group of eight all begin with *bet*, the second letter, and so on throughout the 22 sections of the psalm. Most modern English translations have these eight-verse sections marked in the text of Psalm 119.

THE PRIORITY OF A DEDICATED MIND

Philippians 2:1-11

*In this lesson we discover what it means
to have the same mind as Christ Jesus.*

OUTLINE

Jesus Christ's mind led Him on a path of humility and servanthood,
not a path of pride and self-promotion. If we have the mind of
Christ, then our values, perspective, and priorities will be the same
as His. Our path in life may be different, but we will live our life
the way He lived His.

I.   The Instruction of the Mind of Christ

II. The Illustration of the Mind of Christ
   A. He Relinquished His Place
   B. He Refused His Prerogative
   C. He Renounced His Privileges
   D. He Restricted His Presence
   E. He Realized His Purpose
   F. He Received His Promotion

III. The Implication of the Mind of Christ
   A. The Words of the Old Testament
   B. The Words of Jesus
   C. The Words of the Apostles

IV. The Importance of the Mind of Christ
   A. The Mind of Christ Produces Unity
   B. The Mind of Christ Produces Usefulness

Philippians 2:5 is a central verse in the study of the Christian and his or her mind: "Let this mind be in you which was also in Christ Jesus." The obvious question is, What does it mean to let Christ's mind be in us? Whatever it means (and that is what we will pursue in this lesson), the implications are enormous! The idea that you and I could have the same mind as Jesus Christ is surely a life-changing notion. It is something that should be of the highest priority.

We can say at the outset that Philippians 2:5 does not mean we will become clones of Jesus; we will not become the divine Son of God as He was. It does not mean we will become infallible and sinless after being born again through faith. Rather, in simplest terms, it means we will have the same outlook on life as Christ did. We will look at life through kingdom-colored glasses, gaining a new perspective and appreciation for God's plan of redemption, for God's words and work in the world. We will learn to replace our worldly, fallen point of view with a divine point of view about our purpose in life and God's plan for the ages.

The human mind sets us apart from the rest of God's creation. The mind is what allows us to communicate with God and, aided by the Spirit, understand and apply the will of God in our life. The human mind goes far beyond what any man-made computer can do. It is at once the most powerful and most mysterious aspect of God's creation.

As Paul writes in Ephesians 2, we—along with our mind— were dead in our sins and transgressions. But when we are made alive in Christ by the regenerating power of the Spirit, our mind comes alive, as it were, and gains the ability to communicate with our Creator God. The "natural man does not receive the things of the Spirit of God, for they are foolishness to him" (1 Corinthians 2:14). But we have received "the Spirit who is from God, that we might know the things that have been freely given to us by God" (1 Corinthians 2:12).

Jesus Christ came into this world with a mind alive to God, untainted by sin. Now, Paul says, we are to let that same mind be in us that was in Christ Jesus.

THE INSTRUCTION OF THE MIND OF CHRIST

The most important way to understand the meaning of Philippians 2:5 is by noting its context—the verses that immediately follow. Paul writes, "Let this mind be in you which was also in Christ Jesus, who . . . ." The word "who" introduces us to the person of Christ and the kind of person His mind made Him. By understanding Christ's mind, we can understand who we will be when His mind is in us.

Before looking at the context of Philippians 2:5-11, please note that the word "mind" occurs four times in the early verses of Philippians 2: "like-minded" and being of "one mind" in verse 2, "lowliness of mind" in verse 3, then Christ's "mind" in verse 5. The entire context of Philippians 2 is about the Christian mind—the kind of people we will be when we have the mind of Christ.

Obviously, Christ's mind directed Jesus during His life on earth, just as our mind directs us. Philippians 2 becomes an appendix, of sorts, to the four Gospels because it tells us what Christ "had in mind" during His years on earth.[1] What was His agenda? What were His priorities? What values drove His decisions and actions? When we answer those questions, we understand the mind of Christ. And we will know what it means to let His mind (His agenda, priorities, values and so on) live in us.

THE ILLUSTRATION OF THE MIND OF CHRIST

Paul gives us a lot of information about how and why Jesus came to earth, but not for biographical purposes. Paul is not writing a fifth Gospel in Philippians 2. Rather, his point is to tell us how Jesus lived because that is how we should live when Jesus lives in us (Galatians 2:20). His point is to tell us what it means to have the mind of Christ.

He Relinquished His Place

Christ was "in the form of God" when He came to earth (verse 6). He was "equal with God" (verse 6). As we will see, the attribute of Christ that Paul will focus on is humility. When we realize the place from which Christ came, as God Himself, then humility is the only word adequate to describe His mindset in coming to earth. He came from being God to being the God-Man. While it is difficult for us to comprehend what Christ gave up when He came to earth, it is central to Paul's argument.

Numerous verses in the New Testament, both Christ's words and the words of the apostles, affirm the place of deity from which Christ came: John 14:9, Colossians 1:19, and 1 Timothy 3:16 ("God was manifested in the flesh" in Christ). No one can read the New Testament with an open mind and come to any other conclusion but that Jesus is presented as the God-Man, God in human flesh. The place Christ relinquished when He came to earth was His place in heaven as the Second Person of the Trinity. He did not cease to be divine by coming to earth, but He humbled Himself by relinquishing the prerogatives of His place.

He Refused His Prerogative

Verse 6 says that Christ "did not consider it robbery to be equal with God." Another translation says that Christ "did not consider equality with God something to be grasped" (NIV 1984). As a robber grasps greedily at the object of his desire, so Christ could have grasped greedily at His equality with God. But He refused to do so. He gave up that right in an act of humility.

In order for Christ to come to earth and represent man before the bar of God's justice, He had to set aside His glory and His rights as God and become a man. Rather than grasping and holding onto His divine rights, He surrendered them in humility so as to become one of us. As Paul wrote in 2 Corinthians 8:9, "Though He was rich, yet for your sakes He became poor, that you through His poverty might become rich."

He Renounced His Privileges

What does it mean that Christ "made Himself of no reputation" (verse 7)? One thing it doesn't mean is that Christ ceased to be God. Diminished deity is no deity at all. Christ never ceased to be God.

Rather, it is Paul continuing on the theme of Christ's humility. Christ did not come to earth boasting of His identity as God. Rather, He came in complete and humble dependence on God the Father's will for His life. He lived the same life of faith in God that He knew we would be asked to live. And He did it by relying not on His own attributes or reputation but by relying on the grace of God. The Gospel of John contains a string of verses that illustrate Christ's dependence not on Himself but on the Father: John 5:19, 30; 7:16, 28; 8:28, 50; 14:24. All these verses express Jesus' dependence on the Father for initiative, direction, plans, doctrine, and even the words He was to speak. Jesus gave up His right and prerogative to chart His own course and devise His own plan. Instead, He relied wholly on the Father. In the book of Hebrews we are told that Jesus said, "Behold, I have come … to do Your will, O God" (Hebrews 10:7).

Remember—all these attitudes we are seeing in Christ are indicative of the mind of Christ, the mind Paul says should be in us.

He Restricted His Presence

When Jesus came to earth, He took "the form of a bondservant, and [came] in the likeness of men" (verse 2:7). Nothing is more amazing in all of human history—that the God of the universe willingly came to earth to be born of a human woman as a helpless infant. He could have done anything He pleased, but He chose the lowliest of all ways to present Himself to mankind—as one of us. Jesus is God being born as a human baby and living as one of us for all His earthly life.

A Puritan theologian, Thomas Watson, put it this way:

Christ's taking our flesh was one of the lowest steps of humility. He humbled himself more by lying in the virgin's womb than by hanging on the cross. It was not so much for a man to die, men die, but for God to become man was the wonder of humility. . . . For him to be made flesh who was equal with God—oh what humility! He stood upon even ground with God . . . yet He stripped Himself of the robes of His glory, and covered himself with the rags of humanity.[2]

He Realized His Purpose

In the ultimate sense, Christ was born to die. He came to earth to die as a sacrifice for the sins of humanity—Paul's point in verse 8: "And being found in appearance as a man, He humbled Himself and became obedient to the point of death, even the death of the cross." Jesus made clear that His death was no accident. He said, "For even the Son of Man did not come to be served, but to serve and to give His life a ransom for many" (Mark 10:45).

"The death of the cross" was the ultimate manifestation of humility, a death that was the cruelest in the Roman catalog, a death reserved for non-Roman, common criminals. Jesus humbly submitted Himself to a form of death that no one deserved less.

He Received His Promotion

Finally, the fruit of Jesus' humility was manifested:

Therefore God also has highly exalted Him and given Him the name which is above every name, that at the name of Jesus every knee should bow, of those in heaven, and of those on earth, and of those under the earth, and that every tongue should confess that Jesus Christ is Lord, to the glory of God the Father (verses 9-11).

Someone has said that Philippians 2:5-11 gives us the round trip itinerary of Jesus from heaven to earth and back to heaven. But again, the point is not history, biography, or chronology. The point is the kind of mind that it takes to humble oneself to accomplish the will of God. That is the mind Paul wanted the Philippians to have in themselves.

THE IMPLICATION OF THE MIND OF CHRIST

The mind of Christ was not one of arrogant boasting, a mind of seeking pride of place or position. Rather, it was a mind of humility that embraced God's will as the perfect will for His life. That is the mind that we are to have—the mind which was also in Christ Jesus.

The Words of the Old Testament

The Old Testament is filled with words and examples of the fear of the Lord being the fundamental requirement of those who would live a humble life. Proverbs 15:33 says, "The fear of the Lord is the instruction of wisdom, and before honor is humility." And Proverbs 29:23 says, "A man's pride will bring him low, but the humble in spirit will retain honor." Humility is honored by God— that is the reason God exalted Jesus above all humanity at the end of His life on earth.

The Words of Jesus

Jesus' own words confirm the Old Testament pattern: "Therefore whoever humbles himself as this little child is the greatest in the kingdom of heaven" (Matthew 18:4; see also Luke 14:11; 18:14). Humility comes before greatness or honor.

The Words of the Apostles

One of the most often-quoted verses on this subject is James 4:6: "But He gives more grace. Therefore He says: 'God resists the proud, but gives grace to the humble'"—a quote of Proverbs 3:34 (also quoted in 1 Peter 5:5). Can you imagine the utter futility of trying to accomplish something when the God of the universe is resisting you? God is serious about pride.

The shortest tenure of a member of our church staff was a man whom we hired to do a certain job. That same day, a group of us were setting up chairs for a big meeting that was scheduled—all of us, myself included, were pitching in to get the chairs set up. I noticed the new employee standing off to the side and asked, "Could you give us a hand?" His answer was, "I don't do chairs." Well, he didn't do anything at our church after that since we invited him to find another place to work. When Jesus Christ was humble enough to wash the feet of His disciples, there is no job that any of us should not be willing to do for Him—including setting up chairs. God resists the proud but gives grace to the humble.

THE IMPORTANCE OF THE MIND OF CHRIST

The story I just related is a good example of what Paul wanted to communicate to the Philippians about the mind of Christ. If we are unwilling to do the kinds of humble things Christ did, then we don't have the mind of Christ.

In order to understand more about the mind of Christ, we need to understand two manifestations of the mind of Christ: unity and usefulness.

The Mind of Christ Produces Unity

Philippians 2:1-2 makes the point that, if we profess to have love and fellowship centered in Christ, we should be "like-minded, having the same love, being of one accord, of one mind." In other words, there should be unity in the body of Christ. Think about it— if every member of the church has the mind of Christ, wouldn't there be unity? Would Christ be having arguments with Himself?

Paul wrote to the Philippians about this because some of the members of the church were not getting along with others. Paul mentions the fact that while he was in prison (he wrote to the Philippians from prison in Rome), he heard that some in the church were preaching in his place out of "selfish ambition" (Philippians 1:15-16). And in Philippians 2:14, he reminds them to "do all things without complaining and disputing." And in 4:2, he encourages two women in the church to stop their dispute and "be of the same mind in the Lord." The key to maintaining unity is humility in the face of God and one another.

I hear of dissension and discord in churches all over the country as I travel around and meet with various people. It almost always boils down to someone wanting his or her way, and too often that is a manifestation of pride. But if Christians have the mind of Christ they will never be in disagreement with one another because Christ does not fight with Himself.

All of us have to swallow our pride at times and decide whether the issue we are concerned about is really important enough to divide the Body of Christ. If the issue is doctrine, the truth of the Word of God, there can be no compromise. But that is rarely the issue in churches today. Most church dissension is over matters of opinion concerning the facilities or the order of worship or the personality of the pastor. Those issues should never divide people who have the mind of Christ. The evidence of a church with the mind of Christ is unity.

The Mind of Christ Produces Usefulness

In addition to unity, the mind of Christ always results in usefulness. Probably referring back to those who were preaching in Paul's absence, he writes, "Let nothing be done through selfish ambition or conceit, but in lowliness of mind let each esteem others better than himself. Let each of you look out not only for his own interests, but also for the interests of others" (verses 3-4).

When we look out for the interests of others, it means we are putting them ahead of ourselves. That means we are being useful to the Body of Christ by helping those in need. But if we are too proud to bend down and help someone who is in need, then we can be sure God resists that kind of person. But the person who is humble enough to look out for the needs of others will receive grace from God to help him continue. God resists the proud but gives grace to the humble.

I know of only two places in the New Testament where we are told to follow the example of Jesus Christ. Obviously, we should follow His example in all things, but I'm referring to two specific passages where we are told to live like Him.

One is 1 Peter 2:21-23, a passage in the context of suffering. Peter says that when we suffer undeservedly, we should follow the example of Christ who also suffered without cause. Instead of retaliating against those who persecuted Him, He entrusted Himself to God's just judgment. And we, Peter says, "should follow His steps" and His example (verse 21).

The second instance is the well-known story of Christ washing the feet of His disciples when he met with them on the night of His arrest. After Jesus washed the disciples' feet, He said to them, "For I have given you an example, that you should do as I have done to you" (John 13:15).

On the way to eat the Passover supper with Jesus that night, the disciples had a discussion, an argument, over who was the greatest disciple among their group. It probably had to do with prominence in the coming kingdom of God—who would have the highest position of authority or the greatest responsibility. It's hard for us to imagine such a discussion in light of what we know was about to happen, but that's what the Bible says. So when they arrived at the room for the meal, there was no servant there to wash the dust off their feet, a tradition of that day and time. In the absence of a servant, people would usually help one another get their feet clean before gathering for the meal where they reclined on the floor around a low table. But having just been involved in a heated discussion over who the greatest disciple was, nobody volunteered to wash the others' feet!

So they went through the whole meal with dirty feet. John 13:2-5 tells us that after the meal was over, Jesus took up a towel and, with a basin of water, began to wash the disciples' feet. The disciples knew exactly what was happening. Their pride had prevented them from washing one another's feet, and now their Lord was doing it for them. Jesus demonstrated to them what humility looks like in action—and what foolish pride looks like.

Jesus did this fully aware of who He was and who they were. John tells us that Jesus was quite aware of what was about to happen (John 13:1). He wanted to correct the notion of pride that had infected His disciples and show them what humility looks like so they would have "the mind of Christ" after His soon departure.

Many scholars believe that Philippians 2:5-11 is actually a hymn written for the early church, incorporated by Paul into His letter, that is based on the event recorded in John 13. Reading Philippians 2 and John 13 together shows how the two overlap beautifully. Philippians 2 becomes a commentary on John 13. And just as Jesus told the disciples that they should wash each other's feet just as He had washed theirs (John 13:14), so Paul says we should have the same mind that was in Christ Jesus.

If the Church takes both the words of Jesus and the words of Paul to heart, then there is nothing we should be unwilling to do for one another. If we have the mind of Christ we will serve one another in unity and usefulness. We will be as humble before one another as Christ was before His disciples and before the whole world when He set aside His glory and took the form of a servant.

That's what Paul meant by "let this mind be in you which was also in Christ Jesus." He meant, have a mind of humility, a mind of service to others. The way up in the kingdom of God is first the way down. We only become great in God's sight by first becoming a servant in the sight of God and others. Christ's mind led Him to humble servanthood. If we are like-minded, we will be humble servants as well.

Notes

1. J. A. Motyer, *The Message of Philippians: Jesus Our Joy* (Downers Grove, IL: InterVarsity Press, 1984), 108-109.
2. Thomas Watson compiled and updated by Patti M. Hummel, *Glorifying God*, (Nashville, TN: Thomas Nelson, 2009), from day October 29.

1. Read Philippians 2:5-11.

   a. What does it mean to be "like-minded"?

   b. To understand the "mind of Christ," list the six ways that Christ illustrated for us His dedication to God's purpose and plan for His life.

      •

      •

      •

      •

      •

      •

2. How would you describe a church, a Christian group, or a family that is like-minded? (Philippians 2:2) How do like-minded Christians handle differences or conflicts?

a. Does like-minded mean that all Christians will agree on everything? Or does it have more to do with how they will disagree? (Philippians 2:3-4)

b. Why does Paul put such a high value on Christian unity? (John 13:35)

c. What kind of impact would the Church of Jesus Christ being like-minded have on the world of nonbelievers?

d. Describe the events in this lesson that show the humility of Christ. (See Matthew 18:4)

e. How would you describe the difference in your understanding of spiritual things before and after knowing Christ? How is your mind different (in terms of purpose, values, priorities, understanding, and so on)? (See 1 Corinthians 2:6-16)

1. Read Philippians 2:5 as a group.

   a. What does it mean to let Christ's mind be in us?

   b. What does the mind of Christ produce? Why is this important?

   c. How will having the mind of Christ affect our outlook on life? How will it affect our interactions with others?

d. With Christ's actions as an illustration, what lesson can we learn from His mindset?

e. If we think like Christ, how will our relationship with God change?

2. Christ maintained His deity while setting aside His divine prerogatives. What does Jesus say in John 14:9 about who people see when they see Him?

a. What fully dwelt in Christ? (Colossians 1:19; 2:9)

b. Who did Paul say was manifested in the flesh of Jesus Christ? (1 Timothy 3:16)

3. How do Jesus' own words in Mark 10:45 parallel Paul's description of Jesus in Philippians 2:7?

a. Why do you suppose Jesus humbled himself while on earth? (Philippians 2:8)

b. What will characterize the life of the Christian who has Christ's mind?

c. What is the most challenging dimension of humility and servant-hood for you?

DID YOU KNOW?

Philippians 2:5-11 is known among theologians as the "kenosis passage," a reference to the most important, and most debated, word in the passage: Greek *kenoo*, a verb that means to empty or to make of no effect. That verb occurs in verse 7 where Paul says Jesus "made Himself of no reputation." Other translations say He "emptied Himself" (NASB) or "made himself nothing" (NIV). The debate among theologians revolves around the "emptying"—of what did Christ empty Himself when he became a human being? That question was answered in this lesson—He emptied Himself not of His deity but of His prerogative to act with the power and glory and rights of deity. Rather, He exchanged His glory for the humility of a servant while maintaining His status as God by which He would qualify as a sinless sacrifice for sin.

THE PRIORITY OF A DILIGENT MIND

1 Peter 1:13; 2 Peter 1:3-10

In this lesson we discover the role of diligence in Christian maturity.

OUTLINE

There are some Christians who never travel very far into the kingdom of God. They remain on the outskirts, choosing not to pursue the riches God has promised them in Christ. In short, they lack diligence. And over time, the lack of diligence becomes visibly evident in their life.

I. The Divine Command

II. The Divine Cooperative

III. The Divine Curriculum
   A. The Curriculum Is Conditional
   B. The Curriculum Is Consecutive
   C. The Curriculum Is Comprehensive

IV. The Divine Consequences
   A. Assurance
   B. Abundance
   C. Authenticity

V. The Divine Contrast
   A. We Will Be Incomplete
   B. We Will Be Ineffective
   C. We Will Be Insincere

VI. The Divine Conclusion
   A. We Will Have a Good Experience on Our Way to Heaven
   B. We Will Have a Glorious Entrance Into Heaven

The well-known British devotional writer, Oswald Chambers, wrote, "God will not make me think like Jesus, I have to do it all by myself; I have to bring every thought under the captivity of the obedience of Christ."[1] That is the sort of personal responsibility advocated by the apostle Peter in one of the key verses for this lesson, 1 Peter 1:13: "Therefore gird up the loins of your mind."

When those in Peter's day needed to free themselves from the entanglement of their robes they would tuck the hems of the robe under their belt, or girdle, worn around the waist. So Peter says we are to get free of entanglements; get ready for battle or for a race; get your mind ready to focus on the task at hand. Instead of girding up our robe, we are to gird up our mind. Peter was acutely aware of the need for Christians to diligently apply their mind to their Christian walk. He said we should have the same mind as Christ (1 Peter 4:1) and that we are to keep our mind "stirred up" regarding our spiritual obligations (2 Peter 3:1).

The girded-up mind, the armed mind, and the stirred-up mind all speak of diligence and determination to keep our mind focused on spiritual priorities. Those phrases remind us that we are to live a proactive life for Christ, not just float through life unaware of what is happening around us. Much has been given to us, and much is required of us (Matthew 13:12; Luke 12:48).

THE DIVINE COMMAND

Three times in his epistles Peter exhorts his readers to be diligent (2 Peter 1:5, 10; 3:14). The word "diligent" actually means "strenuous activity"—as in hard work or strenuous exercise. I have to ask myself: Do I approach my walk with Christ that way? Not stressful, but strenuously? That is, do I work as hard at serving and pleasing Him as I do in other dimensions of my life? It's a good question, worthy of our consideration.

THE DIVINE COOPERATIVE

We learn that our diligence is not a matter of the exertion of our flesh but a divine cooperative with God: "As His divine power has given to us all things that pertain to life and godliness" (2 Peter 1:3). The reason we are to give our all in serving God is that He has given His all to us—everything we need for life and godliness.

In the next verse (verse 4), Peter tells us where these things are to be found—in God's "exceedingly great and precious promises." In the Bible, God has deposited everything we need to live a godly life. Peter's words are along the lines of Paul's words in Philippians 2:12-13. Paul says that we are to "work out [our] own salvation with fear and trembling" while remembering that "it is God who works in [us] both to will and to do for His good pleasure." They are both halves of the equation, both sides of the spiritual coin. We are to work out our salvation while God is at work in us! That is the same as Peter's admonition to be diligent with everything God has given us.

If I owned a gold mine and decided to give it to you, two things would have to happen for it to be of any benefit to you. First, I would have to legally give it to you, and second, you would have to take up the necessary tools to get the gold out of the mine. My gift has made you a wealthy person, but it will be up to you to extract the wealth and benefit from it. In fact, we could say the wealth isn't really yours until you work at possessing what has been given to you.

So it is with the Christian life. God has given everything to us but told us to work out our own salvation, to be diligent about benefitting from the promises of spiritual wealth God has made available to us. Yes, there is a divine command, but there is also a divine cooperative whereby God supplies what we need in order for us to be diligent.

THE DIVINE CURRICULUM

Diligence is only the cornerstone, the beginning. There is an entire curriculum of spiritual attributes that flows from diligence: "But also for this very reason, giving all diligence, add to your faith virtue, to virtue knowledge, to knowledge self-control, to self-control perseverance, to perseverance godliness, to godliness brotherly kindness, and to brotherly kindness love. For if these things are yours and abound, you will be neither barren nor unfruitful in the knowledge of our Lord Jesus Christ" (verses 5-8).

Like almost all lists in the New Testament, this one is not iron-clad; this is not a list of all the attributes of the Christian life. Rather it represents, like Paul's fruit of the Spirit (Galatians 5:22-23), what we should expect in the life of one who is following after Christ.

The Curriculum Is Conditional

Peter's curriculum is conditioned on faith: "giving all diligence, add to your faith." (verse 5). Peter assumes that faith is the starting point; faith is the attribute from which all else flows. Faith in Christ is where the Christian life begins. Without faith, there is nothing on which to build: "For no other foundation can anyone lay than that which is laid, which is Jesus Christ" (1 Corinthians 3:11).

The Curriculum Is Consecutive

Peter's list of attributes may be representative, but they are not accidental. Peter placed them in sequential order for a reason: the list begins with faith and ends with love, the greatest of all virtues (1 Corinthians 13:13). In between are attributes that build on faith until they find their fullest expression in love.

From faith springs virtue—a changed life of goodness and integrity. That happens even before the acquisition of knowledge as the Holy Spirit prompts one to live differently. But then knowledge grows which brings the awareness of the need for self-control, and so on. This curriculum of Peter's reveals what happens when diligence is applied to all the Christian life: faith, virtue, knowledge, self-control, perseverance, godliness, brotherly kindness, love.

The Curriculum Is Comprehensive

Everything we need, Peter writes, is given to us by God—everything for life and godliness. We can't major on one part of the curriculum. It all fits together as it comes from God, and we must receive it all. Sometimes we don't see how one part of the faith or doctrine fits with the rest, but it does. It may take time for us to see and understand, but we allow the time rather than questioning the part we don't understand.

Even after decades of studying and preaching the Word of God, I am continually surprised and enlightened by what I learn. There is no end, in this lifetime, to new insight and understanding as we see how God's revelation to us in His Word fits together. That's another dimension of having the mind of Christ—seeing the big picture of the kingdom of God, how God's ways, words, works, and will all fit together beautifully. We should no more expect to understand it all on the first day than we would expect a toddler to understand college courses. Nowhere is diligence more needed than in our persistent study of, and submission to, the Word of God—asking God for illumination and insight as we go.

THE DIVINE CONSEQUENCES

The result of applying diligence to what God has provided is we "will be neither barren nor unfruitful in the knowledge of our Lord Jesus Christ" (verse 8). We will experience three things:

Assurance

Peter says in verse 8, "For if these things are yours." By "yours" Peter means we have embraced the attributes he listed in the previous verses. When we do that, we discover that those attributes become ours; they begin to characterize our life. Truth only becomes ours when we embrace and obey it—not by listening to the preacher. We can have this ultimate assurance as we embrace the great and precious promises of God and apply ourselves diligently to trusting them and realizing that they are true!

Abundance

Next, Peter says we must not only embrace them, we must abound in them: "For if these things are yours and abound" (verse 8). We don't give these truths mental assent only; we live in them and abound in them daily. We reap what we sow when it comes to diligence (Galatians 6:7).

Authenticity

The result is authenticity: "You will be neither barren nor unfruitful in the knowledge of our Lord Jesus Christ" (verse 8). Something happens when we diligently embrace all that God has provided for us. We become assured of our faith—that our faith has become ours, personally. We begin to bear fruit in abundance as spiritual beings. And as a result of the first two, we become authentic Christians. We become like Christ; we manifest the mind of Christ in what we say and do. And that, after all, is the goal of the Christian life (Romans 8:28-29).

THE DIVINE CONTRAST

Peter then gives us a contrast to the picture of the Christian he has just presented: "For he who lacks these things is shortsighted, even to blindness, and has forgotten that he was cleansed from his old sins" (verse 9). No one can say that the Bible doesn't present all sides. It tells us what to do and what will happen, and what will happen if we don't do what we're supposed to do. If we do not embrace God's provision with diligence . . .

We Will Be Incomplete
("For he who lacks these things . . .")

It is important to realize that Peter is writing to Christians. Therefore, it is possible to be a Christian and "lack these things" —virtue, knowledge, self-control, and all the rest. Making a commitment of faith to Christ begins the Christian life, but it does not guarantee maturity in Christ. That results from diligence on our part. Some Christians remain on the sidelines of the Christian life. They remain incomplete in terms of their growth in maturity.

We Will Be Ineffective
("Shortsighted, even to blindness . . .")

The person who fails to pursue the gifts of God with diligence will be "shortsighted, even to blindness" (verse 9). A shortsighted person (nearsighted, in our modern terms) can only focus on things that are close. Things at a distance appear fuzzy and out of focus. When that happens, perspective suffers. It takes a long view, a distant view, of life to maintain a biblical perspective. The Christian who is focused only on today's wants or needs, today's joys or sorrows, will lead a roller-coaster kind of life—up one day, down the next. It takes a long-distance perspective to keep our eyes on the prize that is ours in Christ.

We Will Be Insincere
("And has forgotten that he was cleansed from his old sins.")

It may seem impossible that someone could forget how his life has changed, forget what it meant to be cleansed from his prior sins. But it happens because people begin to live more and more like they lived before becoming a Christian! Their present life begins to look more like their past life; there is an insincerity in their present walk.

One of the purposes of regular participation in the Lord's Supper is to be continually reminded of the death of Christ: "For as often as you eat this bread and drink this cup, you proclaim the Lord's death till He comes" (1 Corinthians 11:26). We need to be reminded of who we were before we knew Christ so we keep moving forward and don't drift back to that old life.

THE DIVINE CONCLUSION

Finally, there is a divine conclusion to what Peter has said: "Therefore, brethren, be even more diligent to make your call and election sure, for if you do these things you will never stumble; for so an entrance will be supplied to you abundantly into the everlasting kingdom of our Lord and Savior Jesus Christ."

Not just diligence—"even more diligence" is required! Peter wants us to be sure of our standing in Christ and our kingdom inheritance. Peter notes two realities that will be ours if we are diligent to embrace all that God has provided.

We Will Have a Good Experience on Our Way to Heaven ("If you do these things you will never stumble . . .")

The first benefit is that we will "never stumble." That doesn't mean that we will never make mistakes or commit sins. It means that our heavenly destination will remain certain and sure; it means we will never be in doubt of our heavenly calling as we walk through the trials of this earth. The guarantee found in God's great and precious promises will be so real to us that we will never doubt or fall away from the hope we have in Christ.

Note that there is a condition to our never stumbling: "if you do these things" (verse 10). That brings back into focus the dual responsibilities we have mentioned throughout this lesson: God's and ours. God has given us the promises, but it is up to us to embrace them. It is our job to remain in fellowship with Christ and continue pursuing the kingdom of God with all diligence. If we do so, we will never stumble as we follow Christ in this life on earth—meaning we will never lose our confidence in the eternal destiny promised by God. Even if we do momentarily stumble, part of God's promise is to forgive us and restore us to the path as we seek His help (1 John 1:9).

We don't stumble because of what happens in the moment; we stumble because of what didn't happen *before* the moment. I recall Pastor Chuck Swindoll saying that a broken marriage is never the result of a blowout. Rather, it's the result of a slow leak. If we fail to pursue the promises and priorities of God with diligence over the long term, we are setting ourselves up for stumbling. If we fail to keep our heart and mind fully engaged with His Word and will, then just the slightest temptation can move us off course.

I have been around Christians who are not maintaining their fellowship with Christ, and there is nobody more miserable. I think they are even more miserable than a non-Christian. They have tasted the goodness of God and allowed themselves to drift away. They have lost their assurance, abundance, and authenticity in Christ. They know what they should be doing but are not doing it, which only compounds their misery. They haven't lost their salvation, but they have certainly lost the joy of it.

So Peter's advice is to remain diligent (verse 5)—even more diligent (verse 10)! Do what God expects you to do so you will not stumble.

We Will Have a Glorious Entrance Into Heaven
("For so an entrance will be supplied to you abundantly into the everlasting kingdom of our Lord and Savior Jesus Christ.")

What a fitting end to the entire passage—entrance into the everlasting kingdom of Christ! Not only have we not stumbled on the way to eternity, we experience a glorious entrance when we arrive on that day. I've heard it said that some people will arrive at heaven with the smell of smoke on their clothes—and it won't be because they are smokers. The joke means that they have lived their Christian life right on the edge between heaven and hell, never advancing far enough into the kingdom of God to leave the remnants of their former life behind.

Christians need to understand that there is such a thing as an unproductive, unfruitful Christian life. Some would say that anyone living that way is not a genuine Christian; they do not have the Holy Spirit living within them. But I don't believe that's true. I believe it's possible for a genuine, born-again Christian to get off the narrow track that leads deep into the kingdom of God. They are just a Christian who can't seem to commit to a life of discipleship with Christ.

I, for one, do not want to arrive at the entrance to heaven in that situation. I want to enter in not having stumbled and excited about the prospects of eternal fellowship with the Lord. I want my entrance into heaven to be glorious—not glory for me, but glorious as I give glory to God for granting me everything I needed for life and godliness and bringing me safely to my eternal home. I don't want to sneak into heaven by a side door because I suddenly realized

I failed to keep my responsibilities toward God. I want to arrive with joy and thanksgiving to God for bringing me safely home—and for the abundant life He allowed me to experience during my years on earth (John 10:10). But I believe that will only happen if I remain diligent as both Paul and Peter have exhorted me to be.

This is such an important issue for Christians because I believe we are destined for difficult days ahead. Our world has never been in a more perilous place than it is now, and the day may come when things get even more challenging. We have to be ready for that day. And those who are not living diligently now will not know how to endure the storms that may come. It is not popular to be a Christian today, and it may become even more unpopular in the future. So Christians need to be preparing now to ensure that they do not stumble if the storms get even stronger than they are today. God has given us everything—everything!—we need for life and godliness, but it is up to us to embrace His gifts and promises and learn to walk in them while we can.

After going through a particularly challenging period of my life, health-wise, a number of years ago, I read a book by Gordon MacDonald called *The Life God Blesses*. In that book he told the story of an American yachtsman, Michael Plant, who attempted a solo crossing of the Atlantic Ocean in the autumn of 1992.[2] Two weeks into the voyage, contact with Plant was lost. Both Plant and his sailboat had vanished.

People who knew Plant were surprised because his sailboat was "state of the art." It was built of the best materials, had the best technology, and had all the supplies needed for the trans-Atlantic voyage. Plant was totally equipped with the best of everything. So when he went missing, it was a mystery to all who were tracking his trip. Every effort was made to find the boat. Search planes crisscrossed his planned route and airline pilots flying over the Atlantic were told to listen for emergency radio signals that might be beaming up from the ocean below. But nothing was discovered for days.

Then, his sailboat was finally sighted, floating upside down, some 450 miles west of the Azores Islands. Experienced sailors were surprised at the discovery because sailboats do not normally capsize or float upside down. In fact, they are designed to right themselves even if they get swamped and keel over. This is accomplished by a huge weight being affixed to the keel, the central beam beneath the vessel. This weight always makes a sailboat bottom heavy so it will right itself if it leans over. This heavy weight—8,000 pounds in the case of Plant's sailboat—rides beneath the boat below the waterline. To stay upright, there must be more weight below the water line than above it. If that ratio is reversed—or if the weight is removed—a sailboat will flip over due to the weight above the water line—the mast, sails, cabin, equipment, and other gear.

And, when Plant's boat was inspected, that is exactly what had happened. For some unexplained reason, the ballast on Plant's boat was missing, and the vessel could no longer remain upright. When the out-of-sight ballast was no longer there, the boat became vulnerable to any wave or strong wind.

MacDonald's point was obvious. If we do not have an invisible counterweight in our life—a soul deeply rooted and weighted with the promises and provision of God in Christ—then we are subject to the power of the storms and winds that come against us. It's the invisible part of our spiritual life, who we are in our mind and heart that makes the difference in the storms of life. Even if we are knocked down momentarily, we will right ourselves immediately as the years of accumulated faith and promises pull us back upright again. May you be diligent to be so prepared.

Notes

1. Oswald Chambers, *My Utmost for His Highest* (New York: Dodd, Mead and Company, 1935), 166, reading for June 14.

2. Gordon MacDonald, *The Life God Blesses* (Nashville, TN: Thomas Nelson, 1994), 1-5.

1. Read 1 Peter 1:13.

   a. Based on the description of "gird up the loins of your mind" in this lesson, how would you explain this exhortation to a new Christian?

   b. In today's culture, what are the most likely ways for a Christian's mind to become entangled in negative or distracting thoughts?

c. What does the word "fully" in 1 Peter 1:13 suggest about the possibility of mental, and thus spiritual, distractions? What happens when we are not resting "fully" in the grace of God?

2. Peter commanded us to be diligent in his epistles (2 Peter 1:5). In what ways are you diligent in your Christian walk? How much effort do you put into your relationship with Christ, in comparison to other areas in your life?

3. Our diligence is based on our cooperation. How cooperative are you in following God's will for your life? How have you experienced the fruition of His promises due to your diligence to Him?

4. In regards to your diligence, have you ever experienced a time when God did not provide for your needs? If so, why do you think that was? How did that time affect your faith? How did it affect your relationship with Him?

1. Read 2 Peter 1:1-10, and discuss the following questions:

   a. To whom is Peter writing this letter? (verse 1) Why is this important to note in light of verse 9?

   b. How do verses 2-4 provide great hope—that God has made provision for all of our needs in this life?

   c. According to your understanding of Peter's progression in verses 5-7...

      1. How does faith lead to virtue?

2. How does virtue lead to knowledge?

3. How does knowledge help produce self-control?

4. How does self-control produce perseverance?

5. How does perseverance manifest itself as godliness?

6. How does godliness lead to brotherly kindness?

7. Why is love the ultimate manifestation of a mature Christian faith?

d. How does the word "add" (in verse 5) put the responsibility on us for making sure these transitions and transformations become a part of our life?

e. Why must we "abound" in these attributes according to Peter in verse 8?

f. How can a Christian "make [his or her] call and election sure"? (verse 10)

g. How do we know that Peter is not suggesting that our salvation is dependent on our diligence or good works? (verses 1, 3) Who is the source of our salvation?

The Greek word for "diligence" is *spoude* which derives from a Greek verb that meant to hasten or to hurry. That primary sense is seen in verses like Mark 6:25 and Luke 1:39 which describe people going from one place to another "in a hurry." Going somewhere hurriedly conveys a sense of purpose, urgency, and earnestness that informs the meaning of diligence: leading with diligence (Romans 12:8), being fervent rather than lagging behind (Romans 12:11), being earnest (2 Corinthians 7:11), being devoted (1 Corinthians 7:12), being sincere (2 Corinthians 8:8), and making every effort (Jude 3). Using this semantic range of meanings adds to our understanding of what it means to be diligent in pursuit of spiritual maturity.

THE PRIORITY OF A DETERMINED MIND

Colossians 3:1-4

In this lesson we discover the importance of keeping our mind centered on Jesus Christ.

OUTLINE

Christians have to endure unpredictable and perilous times just as non-Christians do—with one significant difference: While the non-Christian keeps his focus on changing world events and circumstances, the Christian stays centered on his past, present, and future position in Christ.

  I. **Stay Centered on Your Identity With Christ**
     A. We Were Crucified With Christ
     B. We Were Buried Together With Christ
     C. We Were Raised Together With Christ
     D. We Are Seated Together With Christ

 II. **Stay Centered on Your Authority With Christ**

III. **Stay Centered on Your Security With Christ**
     A. The Safety of This Life
     B. The Secrecy of This Life

IV. **Stay Centered on Your Destiny With Christ**

 V. **How Can I Stay Centered in Christ?**
     A. By Your Insistence on Priorities
     B. By Your Interest in God's Word
     C. By Your Investment of Your Treasure

I wrote a book in 2008 called *What in the World Is Going On?* in which I detailed ten developments in the world that I feel are related to God's unfolding prophetic timetable. It's now 2019 and I stand by what I wrote eleven years ago—and could add to it. There is no question that life is moving faster and getting more perilous with every year that passes. Paul tells us in 1 Thessalonians 5:1-3 that events in the last days will develop "as labor pains upon a pregnant woman." That means they will grow more frequent and build with more intensity (as every mother can confirm).

Everyone who pays attention to world developments knows we are in that kind of situation today. The question is no longer, "What in the world is going on?" The question now is, "How do I live in the midst of this rapidly changing world?" Surprisingly, the answers to that question are found in the very verses that tell us about end-time events.

The first answer comes from Colossians 3:1-4, our focus in this lesson:

> If then you were raised with Christ, seek those things which are above, where Christ is, sitting at the right hand of God. Set your mind on things above, not on the things on earth. For you died, and your life is hidden with Christ in God. When Christ who is our life appears, then you [also will] appear with Him in glory.

In the last sentence is a reference to the return of Christ: "When Christ . . . appears." In the verses preceding, we find the instructions we need to live in light of Christ's appearing: "Seek those things which are above . . . . Set your mind on things above." Both "seek" and "set" are present tense, imperative verbs in the Greek language, meaning we are to do it continually. Not once, but continually as a lifestyle. These are not suggestions, but commands. They are ongoing, imperative actions for the Christian who lives in the light of Christ's appearing.

The psychologists tell us we should look within. The opportunists tell us we should look around. The optimist says we should look ahead. The pessimist says we should look out. But God says we should look up; we should look above "where Christ is, sitting at the right hand of God."[1] Our mind and heart should be set on heaven, not on earth: "For our citizenship is in heaven, from which we also eagerly wait for the Savior, the Lord Jesus Christ" (Philippians 3:20).

Setting our mind on heaven means we have to think like heaven thinks. Do you think the hosts of heaven are anxious and insecure about the future of planet earth? If they are not, we should not be either. Setting our mind on heaven means we are not upset by the events on earth. Positively, Paul says to set our mind on heaven. Negatively, he says not to set our mind "on the things of earth" (Colossians 3:2). That doesn't mean we ignore life on earth. It simply means we don't look to earth for our security, our comfort, our knowledge, or our hope. For those things we must look to heaven alone.

Psalm 62:10 says, "If riches increase, do not set your heart on them." There is nothing wrong with riches increasing; but if your heart is set on them, you will be devastated if they decrease. Finances are just one part of life that we entrust to the Lord. As stewards, our job is to faithfully use and manage what He supplies, not control the supply to the point of despair if it is taken away. Our focus is on heaven, not on earth.

When I travel internationally, I have a stubborn habit of keeping my watch set on the Pacific Time Zone in the U.S. where I live. If I am halfway around the world, I calculate the time there by knowing what time it is in San Diego, my home base. For the Christian, living in this world is the same. We judge everything around us by the standards of heaven, our home base. We don't adjust our life to match the standards of life on earth. Rather, we conform our life to the standards and expectations of heaven.

If we look closely at Paul's words in Colossians 3:1-4, we will find instructions on how to keep our mind centered on things above.

STAY CENTERED ON YOUR IDENTITY WITH CHRIST

The first word in Colossians 3:1 should be translated "since" rather than "if then": "Since you were raised with Christ." The Greek construction of the sentence implies something that has already happened ("since"), not something that might happen ("if").

"Raised with Christ" is a metaphor that is only part of what it means to be identified with Christ. In fact, we were crucified, buried, and raised with Christ—and are now seated with Him in the heavenlies.

We Were Crucified With Christ

Paul says in Galatians 2:20, "I am crucified with Christ." As Paul explains in more detail in other passages, Paul saw himself (his sins) as having gone to the cross in Christ.

We Were Buried Together With Christ

Romans 6:4 says, "Therefore we were buried with Him through baptism into death." When Christ was buried, Paul said, he came down off the cross in Christ and was buried with Him. In Romans 6:4, Paul says baptism is a picture of that burial.

We Were Raised Together With Christ

In a verse from our key passage in Colossians 3, Paul says Christians "were raised with Christ" (verse 1). Our sins were put on the cross with Christ, we were dead and buried with Christ, and have been raised to new life in Christ through faith in Him. Everything that happened to Christ *physically* happened *spiritually* to everyone who is in Christ by faith.

We Are Seated Together With Christ

Likewise, all who are in Christ spiritually are now seated with Christ at the right hand of the Father: "[God] made us sit together in the heavenly places in Christ Jesus" (verse 6).

Paul used this imagery to convey the truth that what happened to Christ—payment for sin by death, burial, then resurrection and exaltation—has happened to us as well. Not physically, of course, but spiritually. We get "credit" spiritually for what Christ underwent physically in our place—when we place our faith in Him as our Substitute and Savior. The moment we take Christ as Savior, all that He went through for us happens to us: our sins are paid for, we are raised to a new life, and are positionally seated with Christ in heaven. My new life is as a citizen of heaven, not a citizen of earth. I am free from the shackles of sin and death, experiencing the new life that Christ secured for me.

Just as Christ lived on earth but now lives in heaven, so do those who are *in Christ*. That's why our mind should be set on heaven, not on earth, for that is where we now live *in Christ*.

STAY CENTERED ON YOUR AUTHORITY WITH CHRIST

Being completely identified with Christ in His death, burial, resurrection, and ascension, we now have new authority in Christ:

"Seek those things which are above, where Christ is, sitting at the right hand of God" (verse 1).

If Christ is seated at the position of authority—at the right hand of God—then we likewise are sitting at the position of authority in Him. Paul pictures Christ's authority by saying He is seated "far above all principality and power and might and dominion, and every name that is named, not only in this age but also in that which is to come" (Ephesians 1:21). Christ is seated higher than all others; therefore He has authority over all.

From Christ's position of authority, He rules over all as Lord of lords. Everything that happens on earth is under His authority. When we say, "I don't know what will happen when . . . ," we have to remember that Christ does. His authority is all-inclusive and all-encompassing. As the ultimate Authority in heaven and on earth, nothing is outside His knowledge or control.

STAY CENTERED ON YOUR SECURITY WITH CHRIST

Authority leads to security—especially when "your life is hidden with Christ in God" (verse 3). If a hurricane were approaching and you were sitting in a secure bunker buried deep inside the base of a granite mountain, how secure would you feel? Multiply that simple illustration by infinity and you get some idea of what it means to be secure "in Christ." If a granite mountain is immovable, how much more immovable is the Creator of the mountain?

The Safety of This Life

John 10:28-29 contains Jesus' well-known words that no one shall snatch us out of His hand or out of the Father's hand. Jesus had been describing His followers as sheep that belonged to Him. And in a day when stealing sheep was a common practice, He said that no one shall snatch His sheep out of His hand. Even though we are physically alive on this earth, we are spiritually secure in Christ. Nothing happens to us on this earth without Jesus' oversight.

The Secrecy of This Life

There is a sense in which the Christian life is a secret life—meaning it isn't known or understood to the non-Christian world. We can't expect to be understood by those who do not know Christ or understand what the Bible teaches. And so when we live a life centered on heavenly things instead of earthly things, and are criticized or ridiculed for it, we just have to accept that as part of the reality of life for the Christian. Paul wrote that the natural man does not understand the things of the Spirit because he doesn't have the Spirit dwelling in him (1 Corinthians 2:14-16). The Christian has to live a "reminded" life—we need to stay reminded of our identity and security with Christ, and the secret nature of our life where the world is concerned.

STAY CENTERED ON YOUR DESTINY WITH CHRIST

Finally, in the last verse of our key passage, Paul writes, "When Christ who is our life appears, then you also will appear with Him in glory" (verse 4).

In Colossians 3:1-4, Paul covers all the tenses of life. We were crucified, buried, and raised with Christ in the past. We are seated with Him and hidden in Him in the present. And we are going to appear with Him in the future. Christians will have been raptured to be with Christ prior to the Great Tribulation and will return with Him for the establishment of His Millennial Kingdom on earth at the end of the Tribulation.

John Ortberg, in his book *Faith and Doubt*,[2] differentiates between hoping in something and Someone. When we hope in something, we will always be disappointed. A thing can break and a circumstance can turn sour. There is no guarantee that hoping in something will ever produce what we hope for. But when we put our hope in Christ, we will never be disappointed. And the hope we have in our destiny with Christ is a hope that no one can take away from us because no one can keep Christ from that blessed appointment in the future. So while we deal with things and circumstances in this life that inevitably disappoint, our challenge is to keep our mind determined on our destiny with Christ.

The stock market, the decisions of politicians, wars, terrorism, diseases—we can hope all day that these things don't touch our life. But there is no guarantee. Our only certainty is that Someone will appear at the end of the age and gather us to Himself, then appear on earth to establish His kingdom.

HOW CAN I STAY CENTERED IN CHRIST?

Every serious Christian will agree with the truth of what has so far been stated—remaining centered in Christ as the focal point of our security in this world. But what may not be as clear is how. How do we remain centered in Christ? Here are three ways:

By Your Insistence on Priorities

One of the benefits of trials in this life is that they cause us to assess, and often reorder, our priorities. For instance, when I was sick with cancer and would receive invitations to speak at different ministry events, my answer was simply "No." Not because I didn't want to but because I physically couldn't. Whereas I might have had trouble saying "No" when I was well, I had no trouble saying "No" when I was sick. My priorities were very clear.

The Christian's first priority is always the kingdom of God: "But seek first the kingdom of God and His righteousness, and all these things shall be added to you" (Matthew 6:33). But sometimes it's easy for that priority to become blurred and we have to snap it back in focus.

When in London a few years ago I met the son of the great British preacher, G. Campbell Morgan. He gave me some of Morgan's books (he was a prolific author), one of which related how G. Campbell Morgan faced crises that occurred in his life like the threatened German invasion of England. He wrote about the courage needed to face such a threat:

> Men who are strong are always men who are fixed somewhere, who have a conviction from which they cannot be separated by argument, which cannot be changed, whatever the circumstances in which they live. Sometimes these men are very narrow, but they are wonderfully strong; [and] they are singularly obstinate, but they are splendidly dependable. Consequently we always know where to find these men. The fixed heart is the secret of courage. Courage is an affair of the heart. Courage is the consciousness of the heart that is fixed . . . . What, then, shall we do in the day of [fear?] We shall do our duty; the thing that is nearest; the thing we have to do tomorrow morning. We will do that, and do it well; and do it cheerfully. The rest we will leave to Him of sorrow, and suffering, and of the issues. What this nation needs now just as much, [but] perhaps more, than anything else, is the multiplication of strong, quiet souls who are not afraid of evil . . . , even though the Zeppelins may be coming, and will not add to the panic that demoralized, but will do their work.[3]

Morgan was talking about the kind of mentality that allows one to see what is really important and stay focused on it, come what may. In other words, priorities.

By Your Interest in God's Word

Most Christians know the wonderful story of Mary and Martha, the sisters of Lazarus, all of whom were close friends of Jesus (Luke 10:38-42). Martha was the activist sister. (I confess to being a Martha as well.) Martha's are characterized by their desire to solve problems, to fix things, to control situations. Those tendencies have their place, of course—but not always. And Jesus had to correct Martha about her activist tendencies when He visited them in their home.

Prior to Jesus' arrival, and even after He got there, Martha was scurrying about taking care of all the details—getting the house and food ready for Jesus' visit. But when Jesus arrived, Mary did the opposite. She sat down at Jesus' feet and listened to everything He was saying. She was concerned about nothing except what the Master was telling them. And this irritated Martha to no end. She was doing all the work and Mary wasn't helping her at all—and she asked Jesus to please tell her sister to get up and help her with the things that needed to be taken care of.

But Jesus said to her, "Martha, Martha, you are worried and troubled about many things. But one thing is needed, and Mary has chosen that good part, which will not be taken away from her" (verses 41-42). His point was this: Activity is fine, unless it becomes more important than hearing from God and spending time with God. When we lose interest in the Word of God because we are more interested in activity, then we are in danger of losing our centeredness in Christ. Mary wanted nothing more than to sit at the feet of Jesus and listen to His words—and Jesus commended her for that.

We can't sit at Jesus' feet, but we can sit quietly and give attention to His Word. This bit of verse equates the written and living Word of God:

> The Bible is the written Word of God.
> It speaks to us of the living Word of God.
> On every page, on every line
> You will find the Son of God divine.
> If you want to learn to know
> The Kings of Kings,
> If you want to learn all

The heavenly things—

Read the Book, learn the Book

Let the Book teach you![4]

By Your Investment of Your Treasure

When priorities are in focus based on consistent attention to the Word of God, there will be careful investment of our treasure. There is no more clear tie-in to being heavenly minded than this point: "Do not lay up for yourselves treasures on earth . . . but lay up for yourselves treasures in heaven. . . . For where your treasure is, there your heart will be also" (Matthew 6:19-21).

I know of a Christian leader who was raising money for a building for the institution of which he was the leader. He reminded the group he was speaking to, that some of them had committed to give funds for the building but they hadn't followed through. He reminded them, with a smile, that if they had given the money they wouldn't have lost it in the recession that began in the fall of 2008. He was playing with them a bit in good fun, but there was an important point in his words. Money invested in heavenly purposes is never a bad investment; it never loses its value regardless of what the stock market or the economy does.

We can always come up with reasons not to give to God what we have promised or intended. But the main reason to give, as Jesus said, is that our heart will follow our money. That is an inviolable principle of God's economy. If we give toward God, our heart will follow our money into the kingdom of God. Sometimes Christians wonder why they have lost some of their passion for the things of God; they wonder why Jesus is not the center of their heart, mind, and affections. A significant reason might be that they are not giving generously toward God. Where our treasure is, that is where our heart and mind will be. So if our treasure is not being invested in God's kingdom, why would we expect our heart and mind to be centered on the King?

Viktor Frankl was the famous Austrian psychiatrist who survived the brutal Nazi Holocaust. On one particularly difficult day, a fellow prisoner at Auschwitz said to Frankl that he hoped their wives were better off in their camp. Frankl, who had just married his wife nine months before their internment in the camps, began thinking daily of his beautiful young wife, Tilly. In fact, he credited her—though she was in another concentration camp—

with helping him survive: "My mind clung to my wife's image, imagining it with uncanny acuteness . . . I understood how a man who has nothing left in this world may still know bliss if for only a brief moment in the contemplation of his beloved."[5]

If a human being can gain inspiration for living and surviving by staying focused on another mortal human being, how much more should we gain inspiration in this life from staying focused on our Lord Jesus Christ? The words of Isaiah 26:3 come to mind: "You will keep him in perfect peace, whose mind is stayed on You, because he trusts in You."

Notes

1. Adapted from John Phillips, *Exploring Colossians and Philemon: An Expository Commentary* (Grand Rapids: Kregel Publications, 2002), 159,163.

2. John Ortberg, *Faith and Doubt* (Grand Rapids, MI: Zondervan, 2008), 84-85.

3. G. Campbell Morgan, "Of His Kingdom, No End," in *In the Shadow of Grace— The Life and Meditations of G. Campbell Morgan*, compiled and edited by Richard Morgan, Howard Morgan and John Morgan (Grand Rapids, MI: Baker Books, 2007) 76.

4. James MacDonald, *God Wrote a Book* (Wheaton, IL: Crossway Books, 2004), 115.

5. Viktor E. Frankl, *Man's Searching for Meaning* (Boston: Beacon Press, 1992), 48-52.

1. Read Colossians 3:1-4.

   a. What does it mean to you to be seated in Christ at God's right hand? (verse 1; see "Did You Know?" page 104)

   b. What can a Christian do to set his or her mind on "things above"? What does that mean to you? (verse 2)

   c. What things "on the earth" have a tendency to occupy your thoughts and concerns? How do you stay focused on heavenly things in spite of earthly urgencies? (verse 2)

d. If you have "died" in Christ (verse 3), how much should earthly concerns bother you in an ultimate sense?

e. How should a Christian balance taking care of earthly concerns (planning, responding) without falling into worry or insecurity? How do you know when you have moved from being practical and proactive to fretful and fearful?

f. How does the idea of being "hidden" (verse 3) in God relate to your protection from earthly upheavals?

g. If Christ is your life (verse 4), how can things on earth affect your life? How hard is it for you to stay focused on eternal life versus temporal life?

2. Take a moment to reflect on your identity in Christ. Then say a prayer thanking the Lord for His continual love, guidance, and comfort.

GROUP QUESTIONS

1. Read Ephesians 2:4-7 aloud.

   • Compare the death talked about in verse 5 with the death Paul
     mentions in Colossians 3:3. What does each death refer to?

   • How does each kind of death ultimately lead to the same
     place—seated together with Christ in heaven?

2. Review Romans 6:4-6 and discuss the passage together.

- What does baptism by immersion represent? (verse 4)

- What does coming up from the waters of baptism signify? (verse 4)

- What is the implication, regarding sin, of having been "crucified with Him"? (verse 6)

- Since our "old man" is dead (the old self that used to worry about earthly things; verse 6), what should characterize the "newness of life" (verse 4) that we now enjoy?

3. What does John 10:28-29 suggest about our security during the trials we may face on earth?

4. As a group, review the three ways in which we as Christians can remain centered in Christ. Then share how you will implement these ways in your daily walk.

-

•

•

5. Discuss where each of you currently store up your "treasure." Does your treasure need to be reallocated somewhere else? (Matthew 6:19-21)

DID YOU KNOW?

Christ being seated at the "right hand" of God (Colossians 3:1) reflects an ancient metaphor for power and authority. Signet rings (reflecting authority) were worn on the right hand (Jeremiah 22:24) and blessings were bestowed—say from fathers to sons (Genesis 48:14, 17)—by the laying of the right hand. The right hand, or the right side of a king's throne, was the position of honor and therefore authority (Psalm 110:1, 5; Mark 14:62). God delivered Israel by the power of His right hand (Exodus 15:6; Psalm 20:6); and when God withdrew His right hand, defeat was the result (Psalm 74:11). For Christ to be seated at the right hand of God was the ultimate designation of honor and approval (Hebrews 8:1; 10:12; 12:2; 1 Peter 3:22).

THE PRIORITY OF A DISCERNING MIND

Philippians 4:6-9

In this lesson we discover the supernatural solution to worry and anxiety.

OUTLINE

Many people discover peace in some new circumstance related to economics, a relationship, or a change in life situation. But there is no guarantee that peace based on anything in this world will last. The only permanent peace available is the peace of God that comes from the God of peace.

I. **The Problem: Worry**

II. **The Prescription: Prayer**
   A. Prayer
   B. Supplication
   C. Requests
   D. Thanksgiving

III. **The Program: Right Thinking and Right Action**
   A. To Avoid Anxiety, We Must Think Proper Thoughts
   B. To Avoid Anxiety, We Must Do the Proper Things

IV. **The Promise: Peace**
   A. God's Protection
   B. God's Presence
   C. God's Peace

Tom Landry was the first and most famous coach of the Dallas Cowboys football team; he began his coaching career about the time I entered Dallas Theological Seminary. I came to admire him greatly—first, for his coaching skills and later for his outspoken testimony for Christ. Coach Landry was known for his calm demeanor on the sideline during the games. Regardless of what was happening on the field, Coach Landry was composed and collected. Later in his life he revealed the secret to his composure under pressure:

> Most of the athletes who fail to become winners are those athletes whose fears and anxieties prevent them from reaching their potential. I overcame my fears and my anxieties by a commitment to something far greater than winning a football game. I overcame them by my commitment to Jesus Christ.[1]

Most Christians would agree with the coach that Christ is the key to a life of peace. And yet not all Christians live with the peace that can come from knowing Christ. Including, apparently, the Christians in the first-century town of Philippi to whom Paul wrote the letter we call Philippians. The Roman emperor, Nero, was increasing his hostility to Christians all over the Roman Empire, and the Christians in Philippi lived with continual fear of persecution. So Paul included a short paragraph in his letter about finding and keeping peace in the midst of fear and anxiety.

THE PROBLEM: WORRY

Paul begins with an imperative statement: "Be anxious for nothing"—"anxious" being a synonym for "worry." In other words, "Don't worry about anything." It's the same word Jesus used when he described Martha as being "worried and troubled about many things" (Luke 10:41). Martha was worried about "many things," but Paul says not to worry about anything.

Worry has been studied by many researchers over the years, and I have read several reports on these studies. Here's the conclusion: About ninety percent of the things people worry about never happen! Things like health problems, financial problems, calamities, disasters, relationships—we worry about lots of things, and the vast majority of the events we worried would happen, never happen.

But when we worry excessively, the body reacts as if the event had actually happened. The same negative effects on our health from anxiety in an actual stressful situation can happen just from worrying that the event might happen. Your mind sends the same signals to your body when you worry as when you are in an actual stressful situation. Paul didn't know that, of course, yet his exhortation was still exactly what we need: "Be anxious for nothing."

THE PRESCRIPTION: PRAYER

Paul's prescription for peace is prayer: "Be anxious for nothing, but in everything by prayer and supplication, with thanksgiving, let your requests be made known to God" (verse 6). Instead of being anxious for anything, pray about everything. Everything is included in prayer so that everything can be excluded from care! Instead of being filled with care, we are to be occupied with prayer.

Paul takes time to explore the idea of prayer:

Prayer

He uses the broadest, most inclusive word for talking to God—prayer—as a way to introduce the subject. Prayer simply means reverent communication directed toward God, a practice recognized by religious people everywhere. Prayer is a human being talking to God for any number of different reasons.

Supplication

He adds the word "supplication" to expand the general notion of prayer. The Greek word behind supplication means "to entreat." But it means more than just to ask. An entreaty is an energetic, forceful form of asking. Pleading and begging are usually listed as synonyms of entreat. Paul does not imply that sense here, but he does mean that we are to come before God with our needs and make them known.

Requests

The third word is "requests." We come to pray and make entreaty before God, and the requests are those specific things on our list. I have noticed through the years that Christians seem shy about praying specifically. We pray generally—"Lord, bless the missionaries"—but somehow lack the confidence to pray specifically—"Lord, please cause the authorities to grant permission for the new missionary training center to be built before the rainy season begins and halts construction."

I have found that recording my prayers in a journal helps me be specific. When we write, we tend to make lists or bullet points or outlines—and we think more slowly when we write, which helps us to be specific and organized about our "requests." Journaling our prayers also provides a record to which we can refer as God answers our prayers.

Thanksgiving

The fourth word associated with prayer may be the most important of all: with thanksgiving. That phrase deserves to be circled or underlined in our Bibles. Praying "with thanksgiving" changes the entire dynamic of prayer. "With thanksgiving" suggests that, before God even answers our prayer, and however He answers, we have an attitude of gratitude toward Him. It also suggests that we are mindful of all the blessings God has bestowed on us prior to our beginning to pray. We could easily begin every prayer with words of thanksgiving to God for His blessings, His grace, and His mercy toward us.

Often when we pause to pray, we are filled with anxiety over the situation(s) about which we want to pray. But thanksgiving seems to drain that anxiety away. It's hard to thank God for His love and blessings in the past and present and be filled with anxiety about the future. When we realize that the very worst thing that could possibly happen to us in this world is that we could die and go to be with Jesus in heaven—that puts a different light on the things we are worried about. And it is God who has given us the confidence we have about eternal life. So we have every reason to pray, "Lord, thank you that my life is in your hands and my eternal life has been secured by the death and resurrection of Jesus." Thanksgiving puts everything in perspective.

Prayer: Be anxious for nothing, pray about everything, and be thankful for anything and everything God has done for you.

THE PROGRAM: RIGHT THINKING AND RIGHT ACTION

The problem is worry, the prescription is prayer, and the program is two-fold: right thinking and right action.

To Avoid Anxiety, We Must Think Proper Thoughts

Paul gives us eight ways to characterize proper thoughts. We should think about things that are true, noble, just, pure, lovely, edifying (of good report), virtuous, and praiseworthy. Those are things we should "meditate on" (verse 8)—meditate meaning to ponder, consider, and give proper weight and value to.

Whatever Things Are True

Truth obviously means things that are not false. But in the context of worry, truth also means things that are real. We are to live in the realm of reality, not fantasy. So much of worry and anxiety is based on things that are possible, but are not real. Living in denial or in a fantasy world is a form of mental instability or illness. If we limit our thoughts to what is true and what is real or factual, we will worry far less.

Whatever Things Are Noble

Noble things are honorable things. We are more familiar today with the concept of honor than of nobility, but even honor is almost a lost idea. Honor has to do with what is right, good, uplifting, and the like. When someone makes a "noble" gesture, we say he has made a good, elevating attempt to do something above the commonplace. To be that kind of person, we need to have noble and honorable thoughts.

Whatever Things Are Just

Just means righteous by both divine and human standards. Our thoughts should not dwell on unrighteousness but on righteousness.

Whatever Things Are Pure

Philippi was like any other Roman city—there was plenty of opportunity to be touched by moral impurity. Christians of any age are in the same situation, especially in our modern age. Given our exposure to media today, we need to make every effort to avoid anything that leads to impure thoughts.

Whatever Things Are Lovely

The word "lovely" appears only here in the New Testament. It refers to things that were pleasing and attractive both visually and with reference to the life one lives.

Whatever Things Are of Good Report

"Good report" comes from two words that meant "fair speaking" or "good thinking." This pertains to avoiding gossip or negative criticism of others. We should be committed to both getting and giving good reports.

The important thing to note from Paul's words is that we deal with the problem of worry not only by praying and committing things to God but by proper thinking. It is impossible to live a life of peace in our mind if our thoughts are filled with the opposite of the list Paul gave to the Philippians. Because it's impossible not to let bad thoughts into our mind and because we may have spent decades thinking improperly before coming to Christ, we need to know how to replace those negative thoughts with true, noble, just, pure, lovely, and edifying thoughts. And we do that—we "renew" our mind, to use Paul's words in Romans 12:2—through meditating upon the Word of God.

Imagine how challenging that was for the Philippians. All they had was the letter Paul wrote them—possibly they had access to some Old Testament scrolls. But today, there are endless ways for us to saturate our mind with God's Word: Bible reading and study, Scripture memory cards, praise music CDs, sermons on CD and DVD, Christian radio and television, the Bible on your personal digital device, Christian living and theology books and magazines, and the list goes on.

You are probably familiar with the concept of "white noise"—a technology used in many settings today from telephone call centers to headphones that people wear on airplanes. A sound wave signal is generated that cancels out the noise one might otherwise hear. And they work wonderfully! We need the same experience when it comes to the thoughts in our mind—something to cancel out the wrong thoughts and fill that mental space with the kind of thoughts Paul has recommended. The Word of God is our "technology." By filling our mind with God's truth, we leave no space for thoughts that increase the likelihood of anxiety or worry.

Pastor Kent Hughes has rewritten Paul's words in a helpful way: "Finally, brothers, whatever is untrue, whatever is ignoble, whatever is wrong, whatever is impure, whatever is unlovely, whatever is not admirable, if there is anything shoddy or unworthy of praise do not think about these things."[2]

And it is up to us to choose what we think about. I have mentioned already (in a previous lesson) the powerful truth of Isaiah 26:3: "You will keep him in perfect peace, whose mind is stayed on You, because he trusts in You." How does our mind become "stayed" on God? By choosing to think about Him instead of other things. Paul wrote in 2 Corinthians 10:5 that we are responsible to bring "every thought into captivity to the obedience of Christ." When we take responsibility for our thoughts, our mind can be at peace.

To Avoid Anxiety, We Must Do the Proper Things

Not only must we think the proper thoughts to live a worry-free life, we must do the proper things. Paul concluded his paragraph on worry with this admonition: "The things which you learned and received and heard and saw in me, these do, and the God of peace will be with you" (verse 9). He doesn't say, "These think about, talk about, consider, try, or study," he says "these do!"

I went through Philippians once and wrote down everything Paul told the Philippians to do—love one another, be filled with joy, and others. The New Testament is filled with things we as Christians are supposed to do. We must become doers of the Word and not hearers only (James 1:22). When we are busy doing the Word of God, the chance that we will lapse into worry or anxiety is much less. Our mind will be filled, moment by moment, with thoughts of fulfilling the Word of God.

THE PROMISE: PEACE

If we approach the problem of worry with God's prescription of prayer, and implement God's program of thinking and doing, the Bible promises peace: "and the God of peace will be with you" (verse 9).

God's Protection

Paul summarizes the promise at the end of verse 9, but had explained it in more detail in verse 7: "And the peace of God, which surpasses all understanding, will guard your hearts and minds through Christ Jesus." The word "guard" is a Greek verb that means "to garrison." A garrison is like a fort or a military installation where soldiers or armies are housed. So Paul says that the peace of God will become like an army guarding your heart and mind, even in the most challenging of circumstances. The peace of God is there like a guard, standing at the door to deny entrance to thoughts of worry or anxiety.

The Philippians probably had a contingent of Roman soldiers garrisoned in Philippi since their town was the leading Roman city in the district. It was those Roman soldiers that kept the peace—something for which they were famous. So Paul says, "What the Roman soldiers do to keep out troublemakers, so God's peace will do when worry tries to gain entrance to your mind."

God's Presence

To repeat the promise of Paul: "And the God of peace will be with you" (verse 9). In verse 7, Paul talks about the peace of God, and here he talks about the God of peace. Let me illustrate why these are not two different things. If I asked you to choose between having the peace of God and the God of peace, which would you choose? Obviously, you would choose the God of peace. If you have the God who is peace then you also have the peace of God. When you have God, you also have His peace—and all His other attributes like mercy, grace, and love.

When we pray and commit our concerns to God and when we think the right thoughts and do the right things, God is going to be the strongest presence in our life. If we are living our life in complete obedience to Him, He is going to dwell fully in our heart and mind. Now if God is totally with you in every situation of your life, will you have any reason to be fearful, anxious, or worried? No, because the God of peace will be there to meet your needs. As a result of your confidence in Him, you will have His peace—meaning, the peace that characterizes Him. (Reminder: God does not worry or get anxious over "life.")

I have seen this promise validated numerous times as I have watched committed Christian friends go through heart-wrenching situations. These situations would be enough to create anxiety and worry in anyone! But I see them manifest a supernatural kind of peace in the midst of their heartache and concern. They have even said things to me that, paraphrased, sound like this: "Pastor, I don't know how to explain this, but I never sensed the presence of God in my life like I did when I was going through that."

It really doesn't matter what the circumstance is. Perhaps it's the loss of a loved one or the loss of a job, the arrival of a serious illness, or the ending of a marriage. God is not threatened by the things that threaten us. God is with us at every moment and therefore the peace of God is with us as well. God and His peace are not with us more in times of crisis than at other times. But in difficult times, and over a lifetime of walking with Him, we begin to know His presence and His peace in much more intimate ways. In fact, in my experience, the pressure of difficult circumstances seems to push us closer and closer toward God. That's when we realize as never before the meaning of Emmanuel—"God with us."

If you know God through the Lord Jesus Christ today, then God is with you. If you are tempted to worry about a situation or circumstance, you can know that you will not go through that situation alone. The same pressure that pushes a person who doesn't know God away from God (because of bitterness—"Why is God letting this happen?") will push you toward God. You will commit everything to Him, and His peace will guard your heart and mind in Christ Jesus.

God's Peace

The peace of God "surpasses all understanding" (verse 7). Trying to define what that little phrase means almost contradicts the phrase itself. If God's peace is beyond our understanding, then how can we explain it to others? And I think that's exactly what Paul means: You can't explain God's peace in the midst of a crisis or a devastating situation. The best you can do is say, "All I know is that God is here, and that means everything is going to be okay—regardless of what happens."

Sometimes people say they find peace in life based on a change in their circumstances. And that may be true in some measure. But circumstances can change, can't they? There is no peace on this earth based on human or material arrangements that cannot be taken away. The only peace that cannot go away is the peace of God. And that's because the God of peace is immovable. Jesus Himself said, 'Peace I leave with you, My peace I give to you; *not as the world gives do I give to you. Let not your heart be troubled, neither let it be afraid*' (John 14:27, emphasis added). The peace of God is not like the peace of this world.

So there we have an analysis of how to handle the *problem* of worry: the *prescription* of prayer, the *program* of right thinking and doing, and the resulting *promise* of peace: protection and presence of a peace that is nothing like the world can offer.

As I was preaching the messages on which this study guide is based, God gave me a beautiful illustration of what it means to be guarded by the peace of God. I had been to a speaking engagement in Chicago and decided to leave on a 7:00 a.m. flight the next morning. So I rose very early to get to the airport, having gotten very little sleep the night before, only to discover that my flight was delayed. Discovering that the delay would be at least two hours, I went to the airline's lounge area where frequent fliers can relax between flights. I asked the attendant in the lounge if she knew anything about the delay, and she told me to look at her computer screen. She showed me a weather map of Chicago showing a huge red blob—a violent storm —stalled directly over the city of Chicago. Chicago, and the airport, was right in the middle of a terrible storm. That was obviously the cause of the delay.

So she said she would keep me updated, and I found a seat where I could get some work done on my laptop computer. As I worked, I noticed through the wall of glass windows that even though the sun was up, it was still completely dark outside. And the rain began coming down in sheets, beating against the windows. It was not a pretty sight. And all I could think was, "I'm glad I'm not in an airplane right now!"

And then it hit me. There was a massive, violent storm all around me. Wind and rain were pounding against the terminal where I sat. I was surrounded by dangerous weather. Yet there I sat —completely dry, totally safe, sipping on a cup of coffee and working on my computer. I was in the center of a storm but was completely untouched by it all. Why? Because I was in the shelter of the building. I was protected and sheltered—guarded—from the storm raging around me.

That is exactly what happens to those who are protected by the peace of God when the storms of life hit. We commit ourselves to Him in prayer, we submit our requests, and we center our thoughts and our actions on Him. In return, we are given the protection and shelter of the peace of God. We don't know how it works or how it happens. We only know it does. The storm doesn't stop; it continues raging "outside" of our shelter. But it doesn't touch us and we don't worry.

If you are tempted to worry today because of a storm that is raging around you, employ God's prescription and program. Commit your concerns to God in prayer and then expect that the peace of God, beyond your understanding, will guard and shelter your heart and mind in Christ.

Notes

1. Howard E. Ferguson, *The Edge* (Cleveland: Getting the Edge, Co., 1983), 4:9.
2. R. Kent Hughes, *The Disciplines of a Godly Man* (Wheaton, Illinois: Crossway, 1991), 72-73.

1. From Paul's list of the things we should meditate on (Philippians 4:8), use your own words to make a list of their opposites—the things on which we shouldn't dwell.

Think on these things: Don't think on these things:

a. true

b. noble

c. just

d. pure

e. lovely

f. of good report

g. virtuous

h. praiseworthy

2. Paul commanded the people of Philippi to "be anxious for nothing" (Philippians 4:6). How would you define the line that exists between concern and worry?

a. How do you know when you have crossed that line?

b. What are the warning indicators for you?

c. How often do the things you worry about come to fruition? In what way is your body affected by such worry? How is your spiritual life affected?

d. What "red flags" could warn any Christian that they have moved from concern to worry?

3. When struggling with worry, do you often pray? If so, in what way has prayer been helpful to you in combating your worry?

a. When praying, do you make your needs and requests known to God?

b. Do you pray with supplication and with thanksgiving to Him?

1. Based on this lesson, there are two ways to avoid anxiety: to think proper thoughts and to do proper things. In an open dialogue, ask each person to share which proper thought, as described by Paul in Philippians 4:8, is the hardest to meditate on. Then conversely, share which is the easiest.

   a. Why do you suppose thinking proper thoughts helps to eliminate anxiety?

   b. How would you describe things that are "of good report" in our world today?

c. We are commanded to also "do" the things that we are to meditate on. If we are busy living out our proper thoughts, how can we be free from worry?

2. Discuss how the peace of God can qualify as an immediate answer to prayer even though we are praying for other things? (Philippians 4:6-7)

a. Why does peace come after we pray? What does prayer accomplish that makes the situation different than before we prayed?

b. What responsibilities do we have in maintaining peace after we pray and commit everything to God?

c. What should you do if you pray and don't feel "peaceful"? Is peace a feeling or a fact? Or both?

3. Take a few minutes to individually seek the Lord today for His protection, presence, and peace.

DID YOU KNOW?

If you have a copy of the Authorized (King James) Version of the Bible, you may discover that it says "be careful" for nothing in Philippians 4:6 (instead of the NKJV's "be anxious for nothing"). "Careful" is an Old English rendering of the Greek *merimnao* ("be anxious"), and one can see a connection between careful and worry. When we are careful, we examine things closely and in detail. But too much carefulness, too much focus on details and "what if's?", can easily become worry—especially when the "care" we are exercising concerns things not within our control. *Merimnao* is connected to *meris*, a "part" or "portion," and possibly *nous*, or "mind." Therefore, to be anxious is to have a divided mind, a mind that is unsettled.

THE PRIORITY OF A DISCIPLINED MIND

Romans 12:2

*In this lesson we discover the key element
in spiritual transformation.*

OUTLINE

While "all Scripture is profitable," one verse tells how to make progress in spiritual maturity and live out God's perfect will. Romans 12:2 reveals that our life is transformed as our mind is renewed by the Spirit of God using the Word of God to renovate our mind from the inside out.

I. The Purpose of the Renewed Mind
   A. So That We Do Not Become Conformed to This World
   B. So That We Do Become Transformed by the Word

II. The Process of a Renewed Mind
   A. The Two Agents Involved in the Renewal of the Mind
   B. The Two Actions Involved in the Renewal of the Mind
   C. The Two Attitudes Involved in the Renewal of the Mind

III. The Proof of the Renewed Mind
   A. We Will Learn the Will of God
   B. We Will Live the Will of God
   C. We Will Love the Will of God

Jonathan Edwards (d. 1758), the third president of Princeton University, was arguably the greatest theologian in American church history. One of his daughter's, however, was an ongoing test for the great man—she had an uncontrollable temper. When a commendable young man came to Edwards to ask for this daughter's hand in marriage, he refused: "Because she is not worthy of you," Edwards told the suitor. When the young man protested on the grounds of his beloved being a Christian, and therefore suitable for him in marriage, Edwards said, "Young man, she is a Christian, but the grace of God can live with some people with whom no one else ever could."[1]

The problem with Edwards' daughter was that she was a Christian who had not matured. Paul, in the key verse for this lesson, Romans 12:2, tells us how spiritual transformation is to take place—by renewing the mind. New Testament scholar Grant Osborne has said,

> It is clear that the mind is where spiritual growth occurs, and in the mind decisions are made that determine one's spiritual direction and destiny. . . . In other words, the ongoing conduct of the believer is based on input from the world or from God. This will determine whether you live victorious or whether you live in defeat.[2]

There is no more fitting verse on which to focus as we conclude this study on the Christian mind than Romans 12:2.

THE PURPOSE OF THE RENEWED MIND

There are two purposes for renewing the mind—one defensive and one offensive. Defensively, we do not want our mind to be conformed to the world. Offensively, we want our mind to be transformed so that we increasingly gain the mind of Christ.

So That We Do Not Become Conformed to This World

When we become a Christian, our fallen, depraved mind does not disappear. If it did, there would be no choices to make going forward. But the old mind and the new mind of Christ are both present; the old nature and the new nature are together. Therefore, we must choose not to feed the fallen mind with what had nurtured it before we came to Christ—the words, works, and ways of a fallen world.

Paul's word "conformed" ("And do not be conformed to this world") refers to the pressure of an external force, not a conformation that comes from within. I quoted in Lesson 1 of this study guide, the translation of J. B. Phillips which captures the meaning precisely: "Don't let the world around you squeeze you into its own mould . . ." (*The New Testament in Modern English*). And Greek scholar Kenneth Wuest rendered Romans 12:2 this way: "Stop assuming an outward expression which is patterned after this world, an expression which does not come from within, nor does it represent what you are as a child of God."[3]

By "this world" Paul means the values, standards, priorities, fashions, morals—everything that characterizes a world that does not seek after God. Paul calls it "this present evil age" in Galatians 1:4. We are not to allow that world to force us to become like it instead of like Jesus Christ (Romans 8:29).

So That We Do Become Transformed by the Word

Instead of being conformed to the world, we are to be transformed by the Word. "Transformed" is only used three times in the New Testament to describe two different events (two of the three uses describe the transfiguration of Christ—Matthew 17 and Mark 9). Both Matthew and Mark use the word "transform" to describe what happened to Jesus: "His face shone like the sun, and His clothes became as white as the light" (Matthew 17:2). The inner essence of Jesus showed through His physical body so that He literally radiated the glory of God. He was transformed, or transfigured, before the disciples who were with Him.

The third occurrence is in 2 Corinthians 3:18: "But we all . . . are being transformed into the same image from glory to glory." Paul was discussing the change that happened to Moses when he was with God to receive the Law on Mt. Sinai (Exodus 34:29). When Moses came down from the mountain, "the skin of his face shone" because of meeting with God. The apostle John says that one day the same transformation—or metamorphosis (from Greek *metamorphoo*)—will happen to us when we "meet" with God: "Beloved, now we are children of God; and it has not yet been revealed what we shall be, but we know that when He is revealed, we shall be like Him, for we shall see Him as He is" (1 John 3:2).

One day we will be like Jesus from the inside out. We won't become God, but will be like Christ in His sinless character. We will be completely transformed. But for now, God is moving us in that direction by the transformation of our mind. Instead of our fallen mind, we begin to experience the mind of Christ (1 Corinthians 2:16). One day, every true Christian will stand before God in the likeness of His Son—and our transformation, begun in this life on earth, will be complete.

That's what Paul is moving us toward in Romans 12:2 as the Anglican scholar, W. H. Griffith-Thomas put it:

> The only way to prevent the outward shape of our life from being fashioned like that of the world is to take care that the inward spirit of our being is transformed by the renewing of our mind.[4]

Our challenge, which becomes our choice, is to resist the conforming pressure of the world as we embrace the transforming power of the Word.

THE PROCESS OF A RENEWED MIND

The key to our transformation while on earth is the renewing of the mind. And the fundamental idea in renewal, in both Greek and English, is renovation. When the Bible says to renew your mind, it is talking about the complete renovation or the replacement of what was formerly present in your mind, and you replace it with something better. Some of you may own rental property; when someone moves out and it's time to get ready for a new tenant, you renovate the apartment. You tear out the old materials that do not fit in with the new design. And if you can't find a way to use the old things in the new plan, you throw them out and you replace them with something that does. And this is what happens to us when we have our mind renewed. We take all the stuff that previously occupied our mind, and we replace it with that which is in line with God's plan for our life. . . . When we fill our mind with the Word of God which contains the mind of God, it helps us discover His will for our life.[5]

The Two Agents Involved in the Renewal of the Mind

If we are to be transformed in this life it will only happen by the renewal (renovation) of our mind. But there are two agents involved in that process: the Spirit and the Word.

1. The Holy Spirit (Titus 3:5)

Another occurrence of "renewal" in the New Testament besides Romans 12:2 is Titus 3:5 where Paul talks about "the washing of regeneration and renewing of the Holy Spirit." Paul says that the Holy Spirit is the divine agent in the process of renewal.

2. The Word of God (Romans 12:2)

The other agent is the Word of God as we have seen many times throughout this study. Colossians 3:10 says that when we become Christians we begin to be "renewed in knowledge." And in Ephesians 4:23, Paul says we are "renewed in the spirit of [our] mind." The new knowledge we get as Christians comes, of course, from the Word of God. As we learn the Word of God, our mind is renewed (renovated) from the inside out.

Both agents work together. The Spirit of God uses the Word of God to guide us, correct us, and shape us—to transform us—into the image of Christ. As we take in and apply the written Word of God we become more like the living Word of God, Jesus Christ. That is what it means to have the mind of Christ. The old things pass away and "all things [become] new" (2 Corinthians 5:17).

The Two Actions Involved in the Renewal of the Mind

Besides two agents, there are also two actions involved in renewing the mind. One is from the outside in, and the other is from the inside out.

When we become a Christian, the Word of God is outside of us and needs to get inside. That's the first action. If we are not regularly taking in the Word of God, then our mind will not be renewed and we will not be transformed. But the inside-out action is just as important, and that involves our internal preparation to embrace whatever the Word of God says. If our heart is not prepared to receive the Word and obey it, nothing will happen. The late British scholar John R. W. Stott said it well:

To suppose that salvation lies in a book is as foolish as supposing that health lies in a prescription. When we are ill and the doctor prescribes some medicine for us, does he intend that we should go home with the prescription, read it, study it, and learn it by heart? Or that we should frame it and hang it on our bedroom wall? Or that we should tear it up into fragments and eat little pieces of the prescription three times a day after our meals? The absurdity of these . . . is obvious. The prescription cannot cure us. The whole purpose of a prescription is to get us to go to the chemist, obtain the medicine prescribed and drink it. Now the Bible contains the divine prescription for sin-sick souls. It is the only medicine which can save us from perishing. . . . But we do not worship the Bible as if it could save us; we go to Christ. For the overwhelming purpose of the Bible is to send us to Christ and to persuade us to drink the water of life which He offers.[6]

Both the inside-out and outside-in are important, like the two halves of a pair of scissors. We must take in the Word; but if our heart is not prepared to receive it, then it just amounts to historical and devotional information. The Word of God is alive and must be welcomed and embraced for it to do its work (Hebrews 4:12). God usually uses some circumstance in our life to make us say, "I need God's help!" And when that need arises in us, the Word can do its work.

Besides two agents and two actions, there are also two attitudes required.

The Two Attitudes Involved in the Renewal of the Mind

The renewing of the mind and resulting transformation requires both a serious and a submissive attitude on our part.

1. A Serious Attitude

An insight from Greek grammar helps us here: The word for "be transformed" in Romans 12:2 is in the Greek present tense. That means it is intended to be an ongoing process, not a one-time event. "Keep on being transformed" is how we could read it. As Paul wrote in 2 Corinthians 4:16, "Even though our outward man is perishing, yet the inward man is [continually] being renewed day by day." Again, in that verse the renewal is written in the present tense, and the ongoing nature of the process is illustrated by the phrase "day by day."

As someone has said, the Christian life is so hard because it is so daily. The world continually tries to conform us on a daily basis. Therefore, we must be in the renewal and transformation process day by day. I read about the epitaph that a Christian planned to put on his gravestone. He wrote, "I saw a sign on a strip of highway once that I would like to have copied on my gravestone. It said, 'End of construction. Thank you for your patience.'" That pictures the renewal process perfectly. It goes on throughout our life and ends the moment we are with Jesus. Until then, we must remain serious about the daily need for renewal.

2. A Submissive Attitude

Another Greek grammatical insight helps us understand the submissive part of our attitude: "Be transformed" is in the present tense, but the passive voice. If the phrase were written in the active voice it would say, "Transform your mind." Instead, it says, "Be transformed." We don't do the transforming; the transforming is done to us by God the Spirit through the agency of the Word of God. Our responsibility is to let the Spirit of God do His work in us, to let the living Word of God change us from the inside out.

THE PROOF OF THE RENEWED MIND

Scripture indicates there are three ways we can know that our mind is being renewed by the Word of God: We will learn, live, and love the will of God.

We Will Learn the Will of God

Everybody wants to know God's will for his or her life (though not all of those people would be completely ready to *do* the will of God if they were to have it revealed). God may choose to make a change in the direction of our life perfectly clear to us in a variety of ways. But more often than not, I believe the will of God is revealed to us over time as our minds are renewed. Circumstances may still be involved, but it is primarily the Spirit's work in us that makes it possible for us to recognize the direction God is leading us. As we begin to think like Christ, the ways and desires of God for us become more and more sensible. Rather than a bright revelation, the will of God becomes a reasonable conclusion.

Paul refers to the will of God as the "good and acceptable and perfect will of God" for us. The more we know of God, the more we will know of His will. The New Living Translation translates Romans 12:2 this way: "Then you will learn to know God's will for you, which is good and pleasing and perfect." This learning process takes time, like the gaining of wisdom. Just as the renewing of our mind happens over time, so does our ability to discern the will of God.

The more we submit to the work of the Spirit in our life, the more we allow the Word of God to rebuild and renovate our mind, the more we will be able to know intuitively what God is up to in our life. We will sense how God is leading us and what He wants us to do. Yes, you could have an "Aha!" moment when something becomes crystal clear to you. For myself, I have not found that to be the case in my life. I have experienced God's leading in my life to be like a shepherd's relationship with his sheep. My job, as a sheep, is simply to stay close to my Shepherd and follow where He leads. And trust that every place He leads is good, acceptable, and perfect. When I do that for lots of days over a lifetime, I discover I have been in the perfect will of God for my life.

We Will Live the Will of God

The word in this point is "prove"—we will "prove" what the will of God is. We do what we believe is "good and acceptable and perfect" in God's sight and discover that God blesses it, and that it is, indeed, His will. We start by obeying those things in Scripture that are God's will for every follower of Christ. We obey the commands of Scripture not because we are desperately seeking God's particular will for us but because it our responsibility as a servant of Christ. As we are faithful in those "little" things, we discover that God gives us "much," and we respond faithfully. Looking back on our path, we see that God is blessing what He has given us to do. We have "proven" what God's will is. We may not be able to prove it to anyone else, but we know it is God's will for us. And we continue walking in it and proving it. If the blessing ceases or we become uneasy about what we are doing, we stop and seek the Lord. God is just as capable of communicating that something is not His will as He is communicating what is His will. So we walk by faith as our ever-renewing mind becomes more adept at discerning His will.

We Will Love the Will of God

Finally, we prove to ourselves that our mind is being renewed by our love for the will of God. I believe with all my heart that living in the will of God is the most blessed place on earth to live.

And the more we experience that reality, the more we will love it and want to stay in that same place. And the less we will want to go back to the world from which we came. When we experience the transformation that comes with the renewing of our mind, the more defensive we will be about being conformed to this world—about being squeezed into the mold of this world. The pleasures of this world, and whatever affection we might once have held for them, cannot compare to the pleasure of living in the presence of God. Yes, there are detours and setbacks and the occasional wrong turn. But over the long run, we discover that we truly love the life that is lived in doing the will of God. Who wouldn't love something that is "good and acceptable and perfect"?

I know some Christians have regrets as they look back over their life, thinking about what might have been. But I don't believe we have to think that way. If we are living our life, day by day, intent on knowing and doing God's will, we can be confident that our whole life has been "good and acceptable and perfect." Yes, the years before coming to Christ may hold some regrets; but once we know the Lord, I believe we can live confidently in His will day by day.

I was blessed to have been raised by Christian parents who were confident in God's will for their lives. And I learned from an early age about discerning the will of God. I learned it was possible to know God's leading and be happy in it. I know I am doing the only thing I ever wanted to do—be a pastor and preach the Word of God. I had other complimentary interests along the way—Christian radio, music, and sports, for example. But even those interests were centered on getting the Word of God out. When God made it clear that I was to go to seminary in preparation for pastoral ministry, I knew that was His will. And even though I have been approached with other Christian opportunities along the way, I have never thought they were God's will. So I continue to be happy and blessed in what I know to be God's "good and acceptable and perfect will" for my life.

Isn't it amazing that just one simple verse of Scripture contains so much for us to consider? Nothing is more important to fruitfulness in the Christian life than being transformed by the renewing of our mind through the agencies of the Spirit and Word of God. The two most important things any Christian can do involve the mind: repentance and renewal. Repentance literally means to change your mind, and renewal means to let the Word of

God rebuild it. And both are life-long processes. As we live a repentant life, we are continually changing our mind according to the new truth the Holy Spirit shows us through the Word.

May you begin, or continue, the process of allowing your mind to be renewed so you can be transformed into the image of Christ.

Notes

1. Quoted in R. Kent Hughes, *Colossians and Philemon: The Supremacy of Christ* (Wheaton, IL: Crossway Books, 1989), 98.

2. Grant R. Osborne, D. Stuart Briscoe and Haddon Robinson, consulting editors, *Romans: The IVP New Testament Commentary Series* (Downers Grove, IL: InterVarsity Press, 2004), 321-322.

3. Kenneth Wuest, *Wuest's Word Studies from the Greek New Testament* (Grand Rapids, MI: Eerdmans, 1955), I:206-07.

4. W. H. Griffith Thomas, *St. Paul's Epistle to the Romans* (Grand Rapids, MI: Wm. B. Eerdmans Publishing Co., 1946), 326.

5. Adapted from Jim Matthews, *Saved, but Stuck: 30 Days to Personal Revival* (U.S.A.: Xulon Press, 2004), 98-99.

6. Quoted in Derek Tidball, *The Message of Holiness: The Bible Speaks Today* (Downers Grove, IL: InterVarsity Press, 2010), 222.

1. What, according to this lesson, are the overall purposes of a renewed mind?

2. Not every person or institution in "this world" (Romans 12:2) is manifestly evil. So what is it that Paul wants Christians to avoid being conformed to? If not specific evil behavior, what else?

a. Based on the one who dominates this world (1 John 5:19), why is it reasonable to call it "this present evil age" (Galatians 1:4)?

b. Why does the warning in 1 Corinthians 15:33 apply to the danger of conformity to the world?

c. How is it easy to be deceived about the negative impact of this present age? How does Peter's counsel in 1 Peter 5:8 apply?

d. What are the biggest dangers (temptations) for you when it comes to being conformed to this world?

e. What measures can you use to determine whether you are being conformed to the world or transformed into the image of Christ?

f. How are you, embracing your transformation through the Word?

g. Who in your life would notice if you began to be more like this world? Have you given anyone permission to hold you accountable for progress in your transformation? Should you?

1. Read Romans 8:28-29.

    a. How is the word "purpose" in verse 28 defined by verse 29? What is God's ultimate purpose for the Christian?

    b. Note: The word "conformed" in verse 29 is a different Greek word than the negative "conformed" in Romans 12:2. How does verse 29 help illustrate the transformation process described in Romans 12:2?

c. Why are difficult times, suggested by verse 28, so dependent on the renewing of the mind? Why do we need to be able to think clearly—have the mind of Christ—when things are difficult?

2. In what way is the "renewal" of your mind, a renovation?

3. Discuss the two agents involved in the renewal of the mind. What role does each agent play in your transformation process?

a. The Holy Spirit (Titus 3:5)

b. The Word of God (Romans 12:2)

4. How would you describe the "renewal in knowledge" (see Colossians 3:10) that has changed your life since becoming a Christian?

5. In what ways can we know that our mind is being renewed?

6. Share with the group the ways in which you are renewing your mind and transforming as a Christian on a daily basis.

DID YOU KNOW?

The Greek word for "be transformed" is *matamorphoo*, from which comes our English word "metamorphosis." *Metamorphoo* is a compound word made up of *meta* (a common word in Greek with many meanings, in this case implying "change") and *morphe* ("form"). Therefore, a transformation or metamorphosis is a change in form. The word for "conformed to" is *suschematizo*, another compound Greek word made up of *sun* ("with" or "together with") and *schema* ("figure" or "shape," from which comes our English "scheme"). To be conformed to is to be shaped with or to have the same shape as something else—in the case of Romans 12:2, the shape or appearance of "this present evil age" (Galatians 1:4) or "this world" (Romans 12:2).

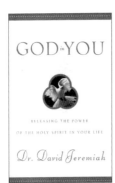

GOD IN YOU

Many Christians find the Holy Spirit the hardest Person of the Holy Trinity to understand. Leaving abstract concepts behind, *God in You* reveals God's Spirit in concrete terms. It brings a fresh, clear understanding of how the Holy Spirit affects our everyday lives as God works in us and with us.

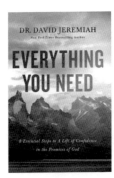

EVERYTHING YOU NEED

God has provided precious promises that provide a clear pathway on how we should live our life today. All we have to do is unpack those promises and discover the essential tools for living a successful Christian life—He has already provided *Everything You Need* for your journey.

Each of these resources was created from a teaching series by Dr. David Jeremiah. Contact Turning Point for more information about correlating materials.

For pricing information and ordering, contact us at

P.O. Box 3838
San Diego, CA 92163
(800) 947-1993
www.DavidJeremiah.org

STAY CONNECTED
to Dr. David Jeremiah

Take advantage of three great ways to let Dr. David Jeremiah
give you spiritual direction every day!

Turning Points Magazine and Devotional

Receive Dr. David Jeremiah's magazine,
Turning Points, each month:
- Thematic study focus
- 48 pages of life-changing reading
- Relevant articles
- Special features
- Daily devotional readings
- Bible study resource offers
- Live event schedule
- Radio & television information

Request *Turning Points* magazine today!
(800) 947-1993 | DavidJeremiah.org/Magazine

Daily Turning Point E-Devotional

Start your day off right! Find words of inspiration
and spiritual motivation waiting for you on
your computer every morning! Receive a daily
e-devotion communication from David Jeremiah
that will strengthen your walk with God and
encourage you to live the authentic Christian life.

Sign up for your free e-devotional today!
www.DavidJeremiah.org/Devo

Turning Point Mobile App

Access Dr. David Jeremiah's video teachings,
audio sermons, and more... whenever and
wherever you are!

Download your free app today!
www.DavidJeremiah.org/App